8 Errors Parents Make

ERRORS
Parents Make
and How to Avoid Them

Michael Brock

CANON PRESS

MOSCOW, IDAHO

Published by Canon Press
P.O. Box 8729, Moscow, Idaho 83843
800.488.2034 | www.canonpress.com

Cover design by Josiah Nance
Interior design and ebook conversion by Valerie Anne Bost

Unless otherwise indicated, Scripture quotations are from the ESV®
Bible (The Holy Bible, English Standard Version®), copyright © 2001
by Crossway. 2011 Text Edition. Used by permission. Scripture quotations marked NIV84 are taken from the Holy Bible, New International
Version®, NIV® Copyright ©1973, 1978, 1984 by Biblica, Inc.® Used by
permission. All rights reserved worldwide.

Printed in the United States of America.

Library of Congress Cataloging-in-Publication Data is on file with the publisher.

24 25 26 27 28 29 30 31 32 33   10 9 8 7 6 5 4 3 2 1

To Lisa, who has given me such a wonderful life,
and with whom it has been a joy to train children.

Contents

Introduction

Lisa and I were sitting on our bed weeping. We had attended a class on child training, arrived home, and started talking. We realized that we had been breaking some very basic training principles, resulting in us too often being frustrated with the behavior of our first two children. It grieved us to know that we had failed our kids. That night consisted of grief and repentance before God. It began a journey to learn and discover all we could about parenting. That was 1995, when we had a five-year-old girl and a two-year-old girl. Now, after adding three more children (another girl and twin boys), I've tried to put in your hands the fruit of that labor.

I wanted to write something that provides general principles and yet is extremely practical. I've found that the parenting books I agree with theologically are often strong on principles but weak on application. On the other hand, books that are strong on practical application sometimes lack the biblical foundation that is needed. This book sifts out the best nuggets of truth from the many books, videos, and seminars my wife and I have learned from, while correcting the theological errors and out-of-balance applications that some of those instructors teach.

This book is similar to the book of Proverbs: it offers general truisms, not promises. There are no formulas guaranteed to produce well-behaved children who love and honor God. But there are mistakes to avoid and Biblical principles to apply. This book lays out many of them.

Though there is a chapter on teenagers, this book is mostly for parents of *young* children, ages one to twelve. This book does not cover infant care.

You need to read the entire book to get the full benefit. Otherwise, you risk missing the general principles that support the specific applications. Not every tool works in every situation. Say you were going to paint your house, and you heard that home improvement stores suggest using "glossy finish." If you went to the store and bought gallons of glossy-finish paint and used it everywhere, you'd have a remarkably ugly house. There are places to use a glossy finish, and there are many more places not to use it. You need to know which is which. The same is true in parenting. You have many tools at your disposal: warnings, spankings, time-outs, naps, etc. The key is knowing when to use each one. If you read this book from beginning to end (rather than just skipping to the sections that you think you need), you'll learn not only how to be a better parent to toddlers or middle schoolers, but how to be a better parent *period*.

I've always said there are two things that people won't let you criticize, and one of them is their parenting philosophy (the other is their "experience" with God; him "speaking" to them). Some parents are hard-nosed and fundamentalist. They tend to only focus on behavior. They are usually strong on rules (girls can't wear makeup, babies shouldn't sleep with Mom or Dad, only homeschool, etc.) but weak on love, warmth, and relationship. Then there are the liberal, natural parents, organic foods and all. They would criticize you for *not* allowing your children to sleep with you; they would also criticize you if you ever bought your kids chicken nuggets from McDonald's. Finally, there are the proud and self-righteous, "I'm not self-righteous" parents who criticize both of these parenting styles. These parents are above the fray of discussing parenting philosophies. They simply want their children to "love Jesus and other people." They refuse to promote any parenting philosophy—except for the one they're actually promoting, the "just focus on Jesus, not rules" philosophy.

This book seeks to correct the imbalances of the first two types of parents while dispelling any sort of self-righteousness in parenting. A teachable, humble parent asks for help from older, successful parents. A teachable, humble parent reads all he can about parenting, listens to all he can, watches everything he can, and attends numerous seminars and workshops to learn about parenting. If your children are disobedient and disrespectful, admit you are doing a poor job, and then go get help. Don't sit around and say, "I've tried that, and it didn't work," or "I guess I just have especially strong-willed children." Those sorts of comments tell me that either you didn't try the right thing or you didn't apply it in the right way. The fact that you are reading a book like this says a lot about your humility and willingness to learn.

This book is divided into a brief biblical foundation, eight errors parents make, and forty-six ways to avoid those errors.

The *Biblical Foundation* is essential because the Bible must be our standard and rule for faith and practice. There are certain paradigms that we need to have correct before we do anything else.

- Error 1 is *Shifting Blame*. Parents must take personal responsibility for their homes and their children's behavior.

- Error 2 covers *Low Expectations*. Parents today seem to have wrong expectations about the whole concept of raising children. I argue that those expectations are unrealistically low.

- Error 3 is having a *Child-Centered Home*. Parents should regularly step back and analyze who or what controls the family. Parents must remember that they are the authority and the leaders in their household.

8 ERRORS PARENTS MAKE

- Error 4 is committed when parents *Fail to Discipline*. Some parents believe that discipline squelches a child's personality, that children should be allowed to express themselves, that discipline creates robots. Nothing could be further from the truth.

- Error 5 is *Reasoning with Your Toddler*. If you're negotiating with your three-year-old, you've lost the battle.

- Error 6 is *Neglecting Your Grade-Schooler*. As your children age, they will need fewer overt acts of discipline. But don't let their physical growth trick you into thinking they don't need your continued involvement in their lives.

- Error 7 is *Disrespecting Your Teenager*. Your teenagers have mature bodies but immature minds. You must remember that and not treat them the way they treat you.

- Error 8 is to *Miss Christ* in this entire process. You can have a child who is obedient and respectful but who, in the long run of life, strays from the Lord, disregards the Scriptures, and never has a heart with Jesus Christ sitting on the throne. This is the ultimate error we must avoid.

I pray the Lord will use this small effort to enable you to overcome the common errors parents make.

Acknowledgments

This book is a compilation of the truths and principles that Lisa and I have learned from others through the years of raising our five children. We owe a debt of gratitude to many. Before I list them, I need to say this: don't throw the baby out with the bathwater when it comes to learning from others about training children. We should learn all we can from faithful Christians, knowing that not everything that comes out of the mouth (or from the pen) of a particular Christian teacher is necessarily true or helpful. There will be some names in this list that some of you will see and think, "Oh yuck, I can't believe Brock likes the teaching of so-and-so. Forget reading this book!" Again, don't throw the baby out with the bathwater. I have some very serious theological disagreements with a number of these folks, but I must admit that I've learned a few things from them in the area of training children. I believe that what I have done in this book is take some of the best teaching from the following sources, filtered out the "bathwater," and left you some good and helpful advice.

With that said, Lisa and I are thankful to the following for all they have taught us (listed in alphabetical order):

1. Reb Bradley. His books were some that we picked up very early in our parenting journey.

2. Dr. Leila Denmark. Dr. Denmark was a pediatrician in the Atlanta area. She was very well known for her professional and practical advice on the care of infants.

3. Gary and Anne Marie Ezzo. The Ezzos ran Growing Families International. We found a number of practical helps in their materials.

4. J. Richard Fugate. His book *What the Bible Says About Child Training* is a classic.

5. Dr. Howard Hendricks. Even before we had children, I remember listening to some talks and sermons by Dr. Hendricks that shaped the way I think about marriage and family life.

6. John MacArthur. Many are familiar with Dr. MacArthur's excellent expositional preaching, but his materials on parenting are very helpful as well.

7. Michael and Debi Pearl. The Pearls and I disagree on a number of systematic theology matters, but they have some keen insights on child training and family life.

8. Neil Postman. Postman was a professor at New York University. He was a secular Jew, not a Christian, but his books on technology

and their negative impact on children and families have been very influential for me.

9. Lou Priolo and Ken Sande. I put these two together because I learned about them at the same time in my life. I have trouble separating who said what. They both have great advice on marriage and family life.

10. The Tripp brothers—Tedd and Paul. Tedd's book *Shepherding a Child's Heart,* and Paul's book on working with teens, *Age of Opportunity*, are wonderful resources.

11. Douglas Wilson. All of his books on family life (especially the ones with the black covers and the paintings) are great.

I had several initial readers in Fairhope, Alabama, give me help with this work. The late Refa Hogue and Emily Chappell were careful to spot spelling errors, misplaced apostrophes, and other grammatical mistakes. Wendy Colbert was invaluable as much more than a "grammar nazi"—she encouraged me, challenged me, and suggested not just rewording some parts but rethinking many sections.

The good folks at Canon Press were kind enough to take on this project, with Ethan Oldham serving as an invaluable editor. I can't overstate how helpful he has been. His attention to detail, challenging questions, helpful suggestions, and gracious demeanor have made this an enjoyable team effort. Thanks, Ethan!

· Of course, I give credit to my wonderful wife Lisa for being such a wise and willing spouse. She is open to the Lord and his Word. She is a learner and a reader, and she has challenged me to think diligently about these issues. She has put it all into practice with great skill and love.

Additionally, I thank my parents for their consistency in disciplining me when I was young. They did this well even before they became Christians! Thanks, Mom and Dad.

A Biblical
Foundation

Lisa and I have watched many friends train their children differently from the way we trained ours. While there were times I could draw a connection between poor adult behavior and poor child training, plenty of our friends' kids are responsible, controlled, civil, and godly, and yet were raised using some different methods than Brock kids were. I am not suggesting that if you don't train children exactly the way I teach in this book, then you are guaranteeing a difficult, rebellious child.

That being said, there *are* biblical principles that must be obeyed. If the following passages in Scripture aren't followed, parents will be clearly going against God's will—and unless God is especially merciful, a difficult, rebellious child will be the result. In this chapter I mention four biblical foundations: Ephesians 6:4, Proverbs 22:15, John 1:14, and Matthew 6:33.

Ephesians 6:4

"Fathers, do not exasperate your children;
instead, bring them up in the training
and instruction of the Lord." NIV84

What does it mean to exasperate your child? The
Greek word we translate into English as "exasperate" is transliterated as *parorgizete*. It means "to
make indignant" or, more broadly, "to vex, to drive
away, to frustrate, and to annoy." The King James
Version translates the verse like this: "Fathers, pro-
voke not your children to wrath: but bring them
up in the nurture and admonition of the Lord."
The idea is that parents are not to foster anger and
hatred in the hearts of their children.

The best way to exasperate your child is by being
easy on them when they're young, and hard on them
when they're old. Too many parents are lenient,
undisciplined, and lax with their children when
they're toddlers, and then crack down on them when
they're teens. Parents can become so enamored with
their "sweet, innocent" children that they let them
get away with almost anything. How many parents
have heard their two-year-old say something sassy,
only to turn their heads and snicker? I understand
the temptation! A two-year-old who exerts her will

is kind of cute, and the trouble she gets herself in is rather small. But as that sassy two-year-old turns twelve, fourteen, and sixteen, it's not so funny anymore. The consequences for her poor decisions intensify. Then the parents start to clamp down and punish—while the spirit of that teenage girl sinks, and the anger in her heart rises toward her parents.

It should be just the opposite. I like to put it this way: *Be hard on your children when they're small and lighten up when they're tall.* Older children are searching for freedom, respect, trust, and independence. If you're clamping down at this point, you will exasperate them. You should be able to give them more freedom and privileges as they grow up. They should sense that you trust them. But this sort of freedom and trust is only possible if they show signs of maturity, and they will only show signs of maturity if parents have taught them to practice self-control. Your kids will certainly not exhibit maturity if you've let them get away with murder from the time they were young. So don't exasperate your child. Be a strict and firm disciplinarian when they're small, so you can lighten up when they're tall.

The next part of this verse from Ephesians tells us to bring up our children in "the nurture and admonition of the Lord." We need to remember the context of the situation in Ephesus when we think about this verse. Ephesus was a Roman province. The people there had been raised in the ways, manners, customs, and mindset of Rome. Paul is teaching that this value system is not proper for Christians. Children are to be raised *in the Lord*—in the ways, manners, customs, and mindset of Jesus. Bible-based values should dominate your home; you should be leading your children to Christ.

The Greek words used here are *paideia* ("nurture") and *nouthesia* ("admonition"). These two words are very broad. *Paideia* is used in Hebrews 12:5–7:

> Have you forgotten the exhortation that addresses you as sons? 'My son, do not regard lightly the discipline (*paideia*) of the Lord, nor be weary when reproved by him. For the Lord disciplines (*paideia*) the one he loves, and chastises every son whom he receives.' It is for discipline (*paideia*) that you have to endure. God is treating you as sons. For what son is there whom his father does not discipline (*paideia*)?

It is also used in 2 Timothy 3:16: "All Scripture is breathed out by God and profitable for teaching, for reproof, for correction, and for training (*paideia*) in righteousness." *Nouthesia*, according to Dr. Martyn Lloyd-Jones, "has reference to words that are spoken"[1] and includes words of exhortation, words

1. D. Martyn Lloyd-Jones, *Life in the Spirit in Marriage, Home, and Work: An Exposition of Ephesians 5:18–6:9* (Grand Rapids: Baker, 1973), 291.

of encouragement, words of reproof, and words of blame. Parents should understand their task covers everything from gentle verbal steering to corporal punishment. Parents can apply these terms in training their children by guiding them with instruction, warning, correcting, and spanking.

Raising your children *in the nurture and admonition of the Lord* should include warmth *and* rigidity, affection *and* firmness.

Strictness without affection often produces children who, despite growing up in a Christian home, reject the Lord. They apostatize because they were presented with a harsh, joyless brand of Christianity, not true Christlike character. Tim Keller once said, "In a society like ours, most people only know of either a very mild, nominal Christianity or a separatist, legalistic Christianity. Neither of these is, may we say, 'the real thing.'"[2] I couldn't agree more. Christianity is not surly, rude, or brutish. So if you're a joyless, grumpy parent, please don't claim to be a Christian. It will make your child hate the Lord. I wouldn't want to be your child, and I'd probably want to do whatever is the opposite of what you want . . . and if you want your child to be a Christian, your child will likely run the opposite

2. Tim Keller, "The Supremacy of Christ and the Gospel in a Postmodern World," Desiring God, September 30, 2006, https://www.desiringgod.org/messages/the-supremacy-of-christ-and -the-gospel-in-a-postmodern-world.

way. Bring them up in the nurture and admonition of the Lord, with the warmth and affection of real Christianity, not the harshness and cruelty of a so-called "Christian" home.

On the other hand, warmth and affection without firmness does not lead to a Jesus-loving, faithful child either. Too many Christian parents think that raising a child in the Lord means they just need to be soft, merciful, and easy. Certainly there are some aspects of Christian parenting that call for these traits. But there are plenty of Christian parents who are quite warm and tender with their children—and are getting run over by their out-of-control, disrespectful household.

The charge to parents from Ephesians 6:4 is to watch out for the hearts of our children. We must protect them from becoming exasperated. We keep them from exasperation when we bring them up in the nurture and admonition of the Lord. And as we see in Hebrews 12, this is the way the Lord brings up all his children.

Proverbs 22:15

"Folly is bound up in the heart of a child, but the rod of discipline drives it far from him."

A Christian parent cannot ignore the Bible's teaching about spanking children. Let me add a few more verses:

> Whoever spares the rod hates his son, but he who loves him is diligent to discipline him. (Prov. 13:24)

> Do not withhold discipline from a child; if you strike him with a rod, he will not die. If you strike him with the rod, you will save his soul from Sheol. (Prov. 23:13–14)

> The rod and reproof give wisdom, but a child left to himself brings shame to his mother. (Prov. 29:15)

The book of Proverbs says a primary tool of the trade in rearing children is spanking. It is one of God's appointed means for training and discipline. To abstain from spanking your child is a recipe for difficulty, disobedience, and disrespect. Not to spank is to say that you know better than God.

Lisa and I were taught and practiced two types of spankings: training swats and traditional spankings. I'll spend more time discussing these two types of spankings in the section on raising toddlers.

Spanking is not the same thing as hitting or beating. To call what I'm calling spanking, "hitting," is to twist the concept into something other than what I'm talking about. It's to use a pejorative term for a concept that is biblical, has been used for thousands of years, and works!

I know that there are some parents reading this book who were abused. I know that there are some parents who never experienced consistent, loving, gentle yet firm, parental discipline. I know that for some, this idea of spanking your children is almost impossible to get your mind around. I feel for you. I really do. I know that this has made training your children much harder and more complex. Take heart. It is very possible to correct your child with corporal punishment both firmly and lovingly. It's very possible to use training swats and spankings with good results, where your children love you and never feel abused or mistreated. By God's grace, you can begin a new chapter in your family history.

Just because something has been misused is not a reason to disregard it. This computer I'm typing on right now is an example. A computer can be misused, from looking at pornography to simply wasting time. But most people would say that this is not reason enough to ban the use of computers entirely. Simply put, computers need to be used properly. And it is the same way with spanking. Just because people misuse the rod doesn't mean we should reject spanking outright—especially since to do so rejects what the Bible says. Again, Proverbs is very clear.

It is interesting to note that in days gone by, people would have thought me strange to defend spanking. They would have wondered why I even have this section in the book. But today, the vogue way of parenting is to avoid the use of the rod. Modern people are supposedly more enlightened and progressive—and they have rejected this old-fashioned, biblical approach. But we must not. Spanking is a primary part of God's way to develop self-controlled, obedient, and enjoyable children.

Rearing of children, like all of life, cannot be done according to the wisdom of the world but rather must be done according to the wisdom of the Bible. We are constantly bombarded with unbiblical messages. We don't even realize the depth of our unbiblical thinking. One of the most popular pieces of worldly wisdom is that good parents leave their children alone and "let them develop into the children God has meant them to be." According to this way of thinking, disciplining your children and requiring them to obey squashes their personality.

But one of the basic premises of the Bible is that your child is a sinner in need of a lot of correction. Remember, Proverbs 22:15 teaches that "folly is bound up in the heart of a child." Genesis 6:5 reads, "The LORD saw that the wickedness of man was great in the earth, and that every intention of the thoughts of his heart was only evil continually." If left to himself, your child will always choose what pleases him and causes harm to himself and others. The spiritual proclivity of every child from birth is to idolize Self (or "be selfish"). It is a fatal error to forget that your child is depraved. It is a fatal error to believe your child is an innocent little angel who simply needs to be left alone to develop as he or she wishes.

Proverbs 23 notes how, when you spank your child, you "save his soul from Sheol." This is a wonderful word of encouragement. Spanking will save your child's soul from Hell. Proverbs 29 mentions, "The rod and reproof give wisdom." Spanking will help your children make better decisions. Spanking is a guide to your children long after they have left your home and are living on their own.

John 1:14

"We have seen his glory, glory as of the only Son from the Father, full of grace and truth."

Typically one parent in a household is more law-oriented, and the other is more grace-oriented. One tends to be lenient and merciful, at times allowing their children to get away with inappropriate behavior. The other tends to be strict and disciplined, at times lacking warmth and affection for their children. It is good and proper for law-oriented parents to feel that maybe they are too demanding. And it's good and proper for grace-oriented parents to feel that maybe they are too permissive. In other words, parents should feel pulled in both directions. Training children requires both compassion *and* high standards. Just as Jesus was *full of grace and truth*.

Parents make a fatal error when they emphasize law over grace, or grace over law. To focus on one end of this spectrum without remembering the other will get you into major trouble.

Law-oriented parents tend to rely exclusively on their authority to lead the relationship with their child. *This is appropriate and important when the child is young* but needs to change as the child matures (more on this in later chapters). One of the problems with this law-emphasizing orientation is that it produces parental nervousness and anxiety. Law-oriented parents are always asking, "Am I doing this right?" We *do* need to be asking this question, and often, especially in the early years. But all of this can lead parents into behaviorism, where they are simply looking for outward conformity to rules.

On the other end of the spectrum, permissive parents focus only on mercy and unity. They scoff at the rules-oriented parents without realizing that they are subconsciously also following a rule: the rule of letting their child have his way so that his personality is not squelched. While law-oriented parents constantly worry whether they are doing things correctly, permissive parents rarely ask that question. But they should. Too often, permissive parents let their child get away with all manner of disobedience and disrespect—they wonder how the child's heart is doing (which is good, but extremely difficult to tell) and bypass looking at his behavior (which is objective, easier to see). The *ultimate* goal is obedience from the heart. But until the child has grown, developed, and understood abstract concepts, simple *obedience* is the goal.

Today's parents tend to be more permissive than in generations past. They need to remember their God-given authority and be a little more law-oriented. Certainly there are horror stories of rigorous and abusive homes, but most of the stories we hear today are of parents getting run over. It is both laughable and heartbreaking to see parents who can't control their thirty-six-inch-tall child. These parents are like a tetherball, swatted around and ill-treated. Their children treat them like servants; they act like their purpose in life is to fulfill their children's wishes.

When your children are older, you will lead them by the power of your relationship. But when they're young, you must lead them by the power of your authority. They will never grow to have any respect for you or appreciate the relationship you have with them if they spend their childhood thinking you are there to do their bidding.

This idea of exhibiting truth and grace in parenting is similar to the way the Lord treats us. He loves us graciously with an undying love, and yet he speaks truth to us that corrects and limits us, for our good and his glory. He is neither harsh, exacting, and unreasonable nor passive, permissive, and weak. We are called to be perfect and love God with all of our heart, soul, mind, and strength—and yet he provides the ability to do so. He gives both the law and the gospel to us. We should do the same for our kids.

Matthew 6:33

"But seek first the kingdom of God and his righteousness, and all these things will be added to you."

The context of this verse is Jesus talking about anxiety. Specifically, he is calling us to not worry about what we are going to eat and what we are going to wear. Food and clothing are obviously important. But Jesus says, essentially, to seek the Lord above all else, and the details of life will fall into place. He teaches us that there's nothing more important than living to honor and please the Lord.

Many parents live for their children and neglect the Lord. They "seek first" their children's success in playing the violin, getting a perfect score on the ACT, or becoming the next Hall of Fame baseball player. But we must live for something bigger than our children. The glory of Christ Jesus and the kingdom of God must be the most important thing in our lives. Of course there are ways we can be so busy "living for God" that we neglect our home life. Children can be made to feel unimportant by parents consumed with church meetings, missionary activities, and ministry efforts. But most parents today have the opposite problem.

For example, consider Christian homeschooling families. We Brocks homeschooled for many years. As a matter of fact, we homeschooled our two oldest girls all the way through high school. We attended seminars and conferences and worked with other homeschool families—we were "all in" and loved it. But I can say from firsthand experience that some homeschool families center their lives around *the family*, to the exclusion of everything else. And as a result, the family suffers. This is because the family was never meant to be the end-all and be-all. God is the end, and the family is one of the means to that end.

A practical way to communicate to your children that your family is focused on God is to say no to some family things so that you can say yes to church things. When you go on vacation, find a local congregation and go worship with them on Sunday rather than sleeping in. Instead of having only family over for Easter lunch, include folks from your church who don't have family in the area. Instead of spending every Saturday going out for a family breakfast at Waffle House or landscaping your lawn, host breakfast for the youth in your church and then go work on the yard of a widow in your church. Attend Sunday school classes and small groups. Give your children the gift of parents who are first and foremost seeking the Lord and His righteousness.

1

ERROR

Shifting Blame

Parenting begins with parents. The biggest problem in your parenting is you. With our biblical foundation in place, it's time to consider eight errors that are common to parents. I've read about these errors, heard about them, and watched friends and acquaintances fall into them over the years. It's time to give some practical advice on avoiding them.

It's tough to hear that the biggest challenge in parenting is parents, because parents tend to be blame-shifters. They come by it honestly. Shifting blame was Adam's response when the Lord confronted him in the Garden of Eden: "The woman whom you gave to me . . ." It is a rare thing to find a person who accepts responsibility for their faults, failures, and sins. Shifting blame is an epidemic. Watch the news, and you'll see some professional athlete or politician make a lame attempt at an apology for his wrongdoing by saying, "If I offended anyone . . . I'm sorry," as if the burden is on others not to be offended by his behavior. This is weak. Parents shouldn't think this way.

I appreciate one of the older couples in my church who has a wayward adult child about whom they have said on more than one occasion, "We were too harsh and legalistic when he was young." I appreciate them taking responsibility for their mistakes. If you're serious about raising godly children, you have to be honest with yourself about how your choices are affecting your household. I'll say it again: parenting begins with parents.

Behave like you want your children to behave.

Your character as a parent spills over onto your children. The apple doesn't fall far from the tree. If you are an angry person, your children will be angry. If you are a lazy person, your children will be lazy. If you are a joyful person, your children will be joyful.

Certainly, there are exceptions. Prodigals break the hearts of their godly parents. But, *in general*, your children will turn out loving the things you love, hating the things you hate, and valuing the things you value. How you handle your money, how you respond to a difficult marriage, your basic stance toward God—all of this is absorbed by your children. More is caught than taught.

I can see how much of the way I behave and, especially, how I think about and relate to God is the result of how my parents think about and relate to God. And for that I am thankful to my parents. Although they did not rear me in a Christian home in the early years of my life, when they eventually did become Christians in their mid-thirties, they experienced a significant change in lifestyle. They grew in and maintained a genuine, lively walk with God. And this has greatly affected me. I've got a long way to go in my sanctification, but I can say that I have a genuine walk with God. In many ways, I can thank my parents for that. My parents were not perfect, but there was nothing fake or contrived about their walk with the Lord. Giving your kids a heart for God should be natural and not manufactured. In order for that to happen, you must develop and maintain a strong personal relationship with Jesus Christ.

So be the kind of person you want your children to be. Make a conscious effort to develop Christlike character. 2 Peter 1:5 tells us to "make every effort to supplement your faith with virtue." This means we must take deliberate, intentional steps to grow and change. Seeing the fruits of the Spirit ripen in your own life is the key to seeing them develop in your children.

Dad, if the only time your children ever see you excited is at a football game—guess what? The only thing your children will be excited about is football. Mom, if you say to your thirteen-year-old, "Tell the ticket man you're twelve years old so you can get in free," don't be surprised when he grows up with a high tolerance for lying. You shouldn't expect your children to be passionate about loving the Lord, working hard, and hating sin if you aren't passionate about those things yourself.

ERROR 1
SHIFTING BLAME

The most important thing you can do for your child is to develop your walk with God. Remember Deuteronomy 6:

> "Hear, O Israel: The LORD our God, the LORD is one. You shall love the LORD your God with all your heart and with all your soul and with all your might. And these words that I command you today shall be on your heart. You shall teach them diligently to your children, and shall talk of them when you sit in your house, and when you walk by the way, and when you lie down, and when you rise." (Deut. 6:4–7)

These verses remind us that parents are to love the Lord first and foremost. Proper training of children results from a heart that has an overflowing relationship with Jesus Christ. These verses also remind us that when a parent loves the Lord, he will talk very naturally and openly about spiritual things. In a Christian home, you should hear the parents discussing their Bible reading. You should hear conversations about theology and personal holiness. You should hear the family praying together for church members, neighbors, and missionaries.

You are the key to raising your kids. You can't hope that the children's ministry, youth group, or

Christian school will be the silver bullet, though those things can be very helpful. Kids need parents who are becoming more like Jesus. The sort of fruit produced in your life will be the sort of fruit produced in your children.

Be the authority.

Too many parents lack confidence. By that, I mostly mean parents lack backbone. They're insecure. They lack the guts needed to be the authority in their homes and train their children.

But God has called parents to exercise authority in their homes. Consider how often in Scripture children are commanded to obey their parents:

> Honor your father and your mother, that your days may be long in the land that the Lord your God is giving you. (Exod. 20:12)

> Hear, my son, your father's instruction, and forsake not your mother's teaching. (Prov. 1:8)

> Children, obey your parents in the Lord, for this is right. (Eph. 6:1)

On the other hand, consider God's words to Eli, who failed to control his sons and let them do whatever they wanted: "Why then do you scorn my sacrifices and my offerings that I commanded for my dwelling, and honor your sons above me?" (1 Sam. 2:29).

Someone is going to be the authority in the home. God says it must be the parents, not the children.

This means you need to speak with authority. You can't hesitate or be wishy-washy. You must be bossy, determined, demanding. Kids need you as their parent, not their friend. Don't talk to your children like you will break them if you are too firm. Don't negotiate with them. Let your yes be yes and your no be no. Sure, you can say, "Let me think about it," and then come back later with an answer. But do not let your children debate with you. You are the boss. Your children are not. If you are constantly getting negotiation, arguing, and complaining from your children, it's probably because you're incentivizing it by giving in every time they whine loud enough or twist your arm hard enough.

There have been times I said no to something that my kids wanted, and then decided to change my mind and let them have it. However, because they did a little bit of pouting or whining, I *couldn't* change my mind. If I had let them have what they wanted after they whined and complained, I would have started to get *more* whining and complaining. They would have realized that whining works. At the Brock house, kids who whined or complained never got their way.

The underlying problem here is that parents are nervous, and they want their children to like them. But if your emotional stability depends on your children liking you, you're in for a long, hard road in parenting. Again, parents are called to be parents, not friends. The funny thing is, if you will be a parent while your children are growing up, you will become lifelong friends with them when they become adults.

ERROR 1
SHIFTING BLAME

ACTION

3

Stop nitpicking.

Christian parents want to please God. This is obviously a good thing—but in their effort to please God, Christian parents can become overly focused on rules, forget about the grace and forgiveness that is theirs in Christ, and thus fail to let the joy of the Lord be their strength. Parents must be joyful.

One way you can know that joy is missing in your home is if you are constantly critical and nitpicky. Joyful, contented Christians see the Lord working behind every circumstance and stay calm when their children make a mistake. Unhappy, anxious Christians doubt the Lord and are always pointing out failures. This is a terrible sin of parents, constantly finding fault.

I remember one time we were at one of those all-you-can-eat buffets. While I was at the food trough filling up my plate, I heard a mom snapping at her young son, "Quit touching all the spoons." And three seconds later, "Don't cough on the food." And three seconds later, "Don't stand in that man's way." And three seconds later, "Don't get so much food on your plate." And three seconds later, "Don't spill your drink." It was constant. It was nitpicky. It was heartbreaking. Did the boy never hear a happy, encouraging word? Granted, maybe the mom was having an unusually bad day—I recognize that it was simply a snapshot in time. But imagine how fearful and low the boy must have felt if that's what he heard all the time. We can't do that to our children. Let's "rejoice always" (1 Thess. 5:16), work to encourage our children, and have the joy of the Lord be our strength.

Now, parents are in the training business, so there's a balance to strike here. On the one hand, you don't want to nitpick; on the other hand, you still have to notice their failures and correct, discipline, and teach. The key to having the right response lies in the will of the child. Is your child being defiant? Or is he simply being asked to do something that is beyond his ability? There's a big difference between dealing with a child's disobedience and dealing with a child's weaknesses. For example, if you tell your child to put his toys away, and he stares back at you with rebellion in his eyes, you will want to fight that battle. But if you tell your child to put his toys away, and he picks up too many and spills them all over the house as he takes them to his toybox, let it go. That's not the time to criticize his poor cleaning skills. Fight the battle when you are dealing with an issue of the heart. Don't be overly critical when your children are simply being stretched a little past their capacity.

ERROR 1
SHIFTING BLAME

It seems to me that moms tend to find fault more than dads. I remember talking with a church member lady who was having a teenage daughter rebel in some pretty extreme ways. She asked me what she should do. I think she was expecting me to suggest sending her daughter away to boarding school or something like that. Instead, I told the mother that she needed to quit being so negative, critical, and sarcastic with her daughter. I told her she needed to quit saying things like, "Why do you pick the biggest losers for friends?" or, "Those chips are really going to look good on your hips." (Parents often resort to sarcasm as their kids get older.) She was surprised at my comments. She hadn't considered the problem might be her rather than her daughter. But she appreciated the advice and tried to put it into practice.

Why do moms tend to be particularly prone to a critical spirit? They have an enormous to-do list at all times, and that to-do list is usually centered around the home. If there's one thing children are good at, it's getting in the way of checking things off a to-do list. Children make a mess where Mom is trying to clean. They require her time and attention when she is seeking to do laundry or cook supper. They get sick when she has meetings planned outside the home. As much as possible, moms need to remind themselves that every interruption is the providence of God—and especially when children are small, moms should realize that their children *are* their to-do list. Everything else is secondary. By remembering this, moms can defeat the sin of finding fault and being nitpicky.

Keeping in mind that training their children is their number one priority should lead moms to reduce the number of outside-the-home activities in which they participate. It should lead them to clear events from their calendars so that they lead less harried lives. Even good things like women's Bible studies and feeding the homeless probably need to take a back seat for a time. There is a brief window of opportunity when your children are young that you must take advantage of. Don't miss that window being busy with things that can wait until your children are older.

I think it's perfectionism that makes us so critical and joyless. I remember one time when I was pulling up some old, nasty carpet at our house that needed to be replaced. Some of my kids wanted to help. Of course, five-year-olds are not all that helpful when you're doing home renovation. So I got frustrated. My kids were making my job more difficult. They were making my job take longer. I wished that they were out of my hair.

Then it hit me that, one day, I would long for them to be hanging around my house. I'd be calling them and asking when they could come for a visit. I realized that it was more important for my kids to be with me and see a happy dad than it was for me to be efficient and perfect in my home renovation work. So they "helped," and I smiled, and we laughed . . . and that's the way it should be. If you're going to give your children the freedom to fail, you must be okay with failure. A perfectionist can't do that.

Another thing a nitpicky parent does is fail to acknowledge accomplishments with praise. Be an encouragement to your child. If your child comes home after making a B on a test, don't let the first words out of your mouth be, "Why didn't you make an A?" If your child gets first chair in trombone and announces that he wants to be a musician when he grows up, don't respond with, "Not if you want to make any money." Quit being a cup of cold water and enjoy your kids.

Some of you may be thinking that if you can't be genuinely happy for your kid (for example, if he decides he wants to be a professional basketball player, but all the men in your family are under five foot eight), then you shouldn't say anything at all. You might be thinking, "It's better to be silent than to say something I'll regret." Well, unfortunately, that's not enough. Silence communicates. Learn to speak up and say something cheerful.

Parents who are joyful in the Lord will have children who are joyful in the Lord. So don't constantly berate your children. Get rid of any critical spirit or harsh tone, and pray that God would make you a more and more joyful Christian.

ACTION 4

Prioritize your marriage.

Your marriage must be the priority in your home. The husband–wife relationship comes ahead of the parent–child relationship.

Remember Genesis 2:24: "Therefore a man shall leave his father and his mother and hold fast to his wife, and they shall become one flesh." This teaches that a man becomes "one flesh" with his wife, and vice versa. The parent–child relationship, while obviously significant, is not a "one flesh" relationship. Rather, it is in one sense made to be broken. A child grows and leaves his father and mother to start his own household. The husband–wife relationship, on the other hand, is inextricable. Spouses are united, one flesh. Your marriage predates your children, and it will last long after your children leave the home.

One of the greatest gifts you can give your kids is a strong, loving marriage. They sense it when Mom and Dad love each other. They feel secure and content.

But when Mom and Dad don't love each other, they sense that too. My mom taught middle school for many years (there's a special place in heaven

ERROR 1
SHIFTING BLAME

right next to Jesus for middle school teachers). She could always tell when things weren't going well at home, because a student would start acting up, clamming up, crying easily, or doing poorly on tests. Time and again, a few weeks or months after the student began misbehaving, my mom would learn that their parents were getting a divorce.

Kids need parents who see their marriage as the priority, who protect it, provide for it, and keep it strong and tender. As the joy in your marriage increases, the joy in your children will increase. As the security in your marriage increases, the security in your children will increase. As you decrease conflict in marriage, you decrease conflict in parenting. Good marriages make for good parents, which make for good kids.

As your children get older this is especially important. Teenagers wake up one day with a new way of thinking. All of a sudden, they become obsessed with belonging to the "in" group, the group that is cool, fun, unique, and special. The last thing in the world they want is to be a part of the loser club. Your home is a club that, by default, they are members of. If your marriage is a loser, then your teenagers will want to get as far away from you and your marriage as possible. But if your marriage is happy and stable, your kids will want to stick around. A beautiful marriage makes your kids proud to belong to your family.

ERROR 1
SHIFTING BLAME

ACTION 5

Show your children that Mom and Dad like each other.

Practically, how can you show your kids your marriage is the priority in the home? Let me mention several ways:

Dates. Regular dates are encouraged by just about every marriage counselor and family therapist. This is not new. Spend time together without your children. Make it a big deal that they get left behind. If your kids are with you 24/7, you're teaching them that they are more important than your marriage. Make sure they know that Mom and Dad still want to be alone together like a couple of teenagers in love. (Sidenote: be sure not to spend all of your date time discussing the kids! That defeats the whole point.)

Couch time. If I remember correctly, the Ezzos introduced us to this concept. It means that when Dad gets home from work at the end of the day, before he does much of anything else, he sits down with Mom for fifteen minutes or so in the middle

ERROR 1
SHIFTING BLAME

of the house, and they talk. The kids can't interrupt. It's time for the husband and wife to visit. Yes,
this requires kids who aren't demanding and can
be alone for a while (in future chapters, I'll have
some suggestions for how to train your children to
be this way). But the benefits of couch time are tremendous. It shows your kids, very obviously, that
Mom and Dad like each other, are concerned about
each other, and prioritize each other. Plus, it's a free
mini-date in the middle of the evening!

Mom is queen. While our kids were growing up,
I always said that Lisa was the queen. That meant
she got my attention. I wanted to please her. She
was the delight of my heart. And I announced that
regularly to the kids.

For example, sometimes when we'd eat out, we'd
let the kids vote on where to go. They'd say Chick-
fil-A or Applebee's or wherever (frankly, with five
kids, there'd be five different places mentioned).
Then Lisa would speak. And I'd say, "Well, my
queen wants to go to Chipotle, so Chipotle it is."
I said it with a smile on my face. I laughed about
how great it would be when my daughters became
queens in their own homes someday. The kids
eventually got to the point where they knew their
votes didn't really matter, because they weren't the
queen. (As an aside, there were times when we'd let
the kids pick the restaurant. But it was certainly the
exception and not the rule.) The point was that the

kids knew my wife had my heart, and I went where she wanted to go.

PDA. PDA stands for Public Displays of Affection. Parents should show affection for each other in front of their children. There are many ways to show affection: holding hands, touching each other on the shoulders and neck, and hugging. Howard Hendricks was a professor at Dallas Theological Seminary many years ago. I remember him talking about family life. He told the story about how one time one of his children walked through the house with a neighbor kid while Howard and his wife were standing in the living room hugging. The Hendricks's son said something along the lines of, "Oh great, there they go again!" This son was familiar with seeing his mom and dad hug and kiss. Your kids need to see that warmth and affection. You need to act like you like each other in front of the kids. It will do wonders for their souls!

One way Lisa and I tried to practice this was to play a little game we called *Best Kiss*. In the morning the last kiss was the best kiss. When I left the house each morning, I'd give kisses to all the kids— but Lisa got the last kiss. And I would announce that the last kiss was best and that Lisa was the one who got it. It became somewhat of a game. After I kissed Lisa goodbye, the kids would chase me down, grab my legs, and jump off couches, trying to smack me with a kiss before I got out of the house. Sometimes I'd let them get a kiss in, and they'd proudly announce that *they* had nabbed the best kiss for the day.

The same thing happened when I came home, except this time, the first kiss was best. I wouldn't kiss anyone until I kissed Lisa. Again, I would announce, while I was plowing through kids, that the first kiss was best and that it went to "my honey." The kids would rush to the car and try to get in a kiss before I got to the house. They would try to climb up me as I was walking to Lisa. Often Lisa would participate in the shenanigans by racing the kids to the car to get the "best kiss." It was a lot of fun.

By the way, Lisa was the only one I would kiss on the lips. This was just a personal Brock house thing. There's no Bible verse about it. But it was another simple way to remind the kids that Mom and Dad had something special.

Present a united front.

Be very careful about arguing or disagreeing in front of your children. They need to see like-mindedness between you and your spouse. They need to see a united front. Don't get into an argument in front of your children. When you disagree, either move to the bedroom or simply put a pause on the discussion until later. All you have to say is something like, "Can we finish this conversation after dinner?" Of course, don't say it with a pompous, sarcastic tone!

I know some people will argue that this is both unrealistic and unhelpful. They will say that kids need to learn that disagreeing is okay. Of course, in time, your kids *will* see you disagree—it's inevitable. So make it your *general* practice not to argue in front of them. On those rare occasions when you do have to disagree in front of your kids, make sure it's a mature, civil discussion and not a loud, finger-pointing, stomping-out-of-the-room tirade.

Never belittle your spouse. This is one of the worst things you can do in your home. Your children will disrespect their parent (your spouse) when they hear you disrespect them, whether it's by rolling your eyes at their suggestions or cracking jokes at their expense. Your children must know that their parents are on the same team, that you're pulling for each other, and that you support each other's decisions.

Generally speaking, avoid talking about your differences when you're actively involved in a training or discipline situation. You'll have a much better discussion when you're not in the middle of a battle with your child. It's also a good idea to defer to the parent who has the strongest opinion. If the husband is adamant that a child should be spanked for being selfish with his toys, and the wife is less opinionated, go with the husband's more zealous opinion. If the wife has a strong opinion about how the kids will relate to the neighborhood kids, and the husband is less opinionated, go with the wife's preference.

Compromise is another helpful technique. If the husband wants to homeschool the children, but the wife wants them to learn in a more social setting, you could meet halfway and put them in a private Christian school or co-op program. Compromising is good for the soul.

Finally, submit to the Bible's instructions regarding male headship in the home. At the end of the day, someone must make a decision. According to the Bible, the husband has that authority and responsibility.

A word to single parents, divorced parents, and step-parents

Because of sin, life is messy. This means family relationships can get tricky. Are children with single or divorced parents a lost cause? Are they guaranteed to be delinquents? Certainly not! There are some unique challenges, but all the principles I'll mention in this book don't change. If you follow them, your kids (by God's grace) will grow up secure and disciplined.

If you are divorced and decide to remarry, the number one thing you can do for your children is remarry a godly spouse who loves them. And then that marriage needs to be a top priority in the new home. If your children are the center of your new household, there will be problems. They need to see a biological parent and a step-parent who treat each other with respect. They desperately need to see love. If they didn't see it in the first home properly, be sure to display it in the second one. A godly step-parent is a wonderful blessing to children.

What about single-parent homes where parents don't remarry, or were never married in the first place? You still have a priority relationship. Your priority relationship is with the Lord. You must communicate to your children that you follow the Lord first and foremost, that your relationship with God takes priority over everything else, and that your world doesn't revolve around them. With your parental responsibilities doubled, it will be especially easy to let things like your personal devotions slide. But guard that time. Don't let your kids interrupt your personal devotions. Make a habit of telling your kids that you need to talk to the Lord whenever they ask you for permission to do something and you aren't sure how to answer them. Keep before your kids the idea that they are not first and the world does not revolve around them.

No matter your situation, don't be discouraged. God is in the resurrection business. He's an expert at drawing straight lines with crooked sticks. There is no such thing as a perfect home or a perfect marriage. By the grace of God and the power of the Holy Spirit, he can make something beautiful out of your home.

ERROR

Low Expectations

For some reason, a lot of parents don't expect to enjoy being around their children. The unspoken consensus is that parents must simply endure. A lot of this has to do with phrases like "the terrible twos" or "the teen years," phrases that suggest children are disobedient and disrespectful at certain ages, and there's nothing you can do about it.

Granted, children are sinners, and it's not fun dealing with sin. There will be days when your kids push you to wonder, "What happened to my sweet child?" But those days don't have to outnumber the good days. Children can be enjoyable, obedient, and respectful—even two-year-olds and teenagers.

7

Expect good behavior.

Many parents expect to have difficult children. And then they pass off other parents' well-behaved children as just plain luck.

I can still remember the comments early on in my life as a parent: "Just wait until you have boys." Then we had boys, and the remarks turned to, "Just wait until they're teenagers." Finally, the commenters pulled out the ultimate trump card: "You sure are lucky not to have strong-willed children." It's amazing, really. I've seen single-child parents complain about how they got one "strong-willed" child, while their friends with large, well-behaved families somehow got lucky eleven times in a row. Obedient kids are not a matter of luck. It isn't a matter of God just happening to give one family compliant children and another family strong-willed ones. Don't be one of those parents who comes up with excuse after excuse to justify their unruly household.

Remember Proverbs 22:6: "Train up a child in the way he should go; even when he is old he will not depart from it." This verse assumes children *can* be trained. Obedience and disobedience aren't the luck of the draw. How you train your children determines, in large part, how they behave. You can train your children to be well-behaved.

Granted, there are many aspects of training children. Proverbs 22:6 doesn't teach us that there is a single, simple, step-by-step formula that guarantees success as a parent. Formulas work in math and chemistry, where every input or component will always produce a certain end result. In the world of training children, not every product can be traced back to a specific parental training practice. Children are not machines. If I press the letter *a* on the keyboard of my computer, the letter *a* appears on the screen. Parents often presume that if they put their children in a Christian school or keep their screen time to a minimum, they will have pressed the right buttons to produce well-behaved kids. But children are human beings created by God with unique personalities and character traits. There is no single silver bullet or magic formula to follow that will produce perfect children every time.

That being said, your unique children can be well-behaved children. They can be enjoyable. There are biblical principles to follow, and generally speaking, the difference between an obedient and a disobedient child is whether or not their parents have followed those principles. That's the reason for this book.

ERROR 2
LOW EXPECTATIONS

ACTION 8

Expect first-time obedience.

"First-time obedience" is a phrase I first heard used by the Ezzos. It means that children should obey every command without needing to have it repeated. When you give your children a command, they should obey promptly and with a pleasant attitude. If they don't obey promptly and with a pleasant attitude, they should be disciplined. It's as clear as that.

When you don't expect first-time obedience, you're undermining your authority. Your children realize that your "Do this" or "Don't do that" doesn't really mean "Do this" or "Don't do that." If children do not respect their parent's authority, there's been a major blunder on the parents' part. We want children to love authority and highly regard a parent's word.

Additionally, not teaching first-time obedience tells your child to obey only when your voice reaches a certain pitch or volume. Only then do they know when you've "had it up to here." Only then do they know when their time to disobey is up.

ERROR 2
LOW EXPECTATIONS

And they will hold on to their independence until that time comes. If you don't train your children to obey your first command, you're training them to disobey your commands, *period*.

When you do require first-time obedience, you follow up every instance of non-compliance with some sort of discipline. If you tell your child, "Put that toy down," and he doesn't obey within a couple of seconds, you discipline him. One of the many beauties of this expectation is that you don't blow your top. You calmly tell your child to do something, he doesn't do it, and he is immediately disciplined—and you are calm and composed all the while. It's the repeating, threatening parent who experiences a steady rise in blood pressure when their child disobeys. That's your fault, parent. Parents who get angry should have disciplined their child for his or her disobedience five minutes earlier—but because they chose not to, their blood pressures are going up and their voices are rising as they repeat their commands and threaten. If you're getting mad at your child, it's your fault. It's your fault for not disciplining them upon their first-time disobedience. Don't punish them for your failure. (Also, you shouldn't be agitated by your children's disobedience. If you become agitated, you're most likely taking it personally. Do not take it personally. Foolishness is bound up in the heart of a child, so expect that you're going to have to discipline them.)

ERROR 2
LOW EXPECTATIONS

Some people will think that requiring first-time obedience is harsh or legalistic. But it's actually the opposite. Legalistic parents are only concerned with the *behavior* of their child. Parents who require first-time obedience are concerned with *how* their child obeys. Does the child obey at your first command? That's what we're shooting for, because the goal is the character trait of self-control.

The main problem with threatening and repeating is your emphasis. If you are threatening, repeating, warning, and pleading, your emphasis is on your child's *behavior*; you are threatening them and pleading with them to act a certain way. But you have to think bigger than their current actions. Your emphasis has to be on their long-term character, particularly the character trait of self-control. Think about it. When your child disobeys your first command and the pleas and threats begin, you are in a battle over what the child *does*. The question becomes *who will win?* As long as you are bigger and can eventually pick your children up and cart them off, you will win. But you won't be bigger forever. Therefore, your emphasis must be—*must* be—their character. They must become self-controlled, self-disciplined people so that when they are fourteen, sixteen, and eighteen you can trust that they will do what is right—even when you're not around. Your children will only achieve that if you cultivate their character by requiring first-time obedience.

ERROR 2
LOW EXPECTATIONS   49

Teach first-time obedience.

So, how does a parent teach first-time obedience? This works best if you start early. The earlier the better. I remember the first swat I gave my oldest was when she was about seven or eight months old. We were at the beach, in a hotel. I put her on the bed to change her diaper. She tried to wiggle away. She was grunting and whining. I told her no, but she kept on doing it. So I swatted her with my hand on the back of her upper thigh, just below the diaper. She cried. And she stopped whining. Little swats like that can start when the child is young.

Many parents think they can teach their children obedience through the use of bribes: "If you're good, I'll get you some ice cream!" But bribes teach your children that they should modify their behavior only when it gets them treats, privileges, and rewards. Children raised on bribes learn to value things over relationships. Maybe even worse than that, they learn that the way life works is by performance. Certainly there is a kernel of truth to this: in most work environments, for example, you must perform at a certain level to get a paycheck. But that's not the gospel. In God's economy, the weak and underperforming receive the blessing of God. And we obey, in part, out of gratitude for the salvation we undeserving sinners receive. Rather than bribing children to obey, parents should train children to obey by disciplining them when they don't.

One thing you can do to help out with this first-time obedience rule is to give your children a "heads-up." For example, when you're about to leave the cousins' house, give them a five-minute warning. Then, when the five minutes are up and you say, "Time for us to go. Pick up the toys," there's no excuse if they don't immediately begin to pick up. Discipline should follow.

You need to keep context in mind when you discipline for first-time obedience. Say you tell your son not to get out of bed. If his little brother falls out of his crib and hurts himself, you of course want him to "disobey"—you want him to get out of bed to come tell you. Say you've spent the entire day at Six Flags, and your daughter missed her nap and she's drained from the sun. If you give her a command in the hotel room at 9 p.m. that night, and her response is sluggish . . . be gracious and lenient. I'd be tired and cranky too. Again, the context should play a part in understanding the situation.

One of the best ways to train your children to obey your first command is to *stage opportunities*.

This means you intentionally create situations where you give commands and quickly respond to any disobedience with discipline. Set up a training scenario. You could give your child his favorite toy to play with and tell him that in five minutes he's going to have to put it down on the coffee table. Five minutes later you go to him (with your switch in your back pocket, out of sight) and say that it's time to put the toy away. He should promptly begin walking to the coffee table. If he doesn't, you quickly take your switch and give him a swat. It should sting. He will cry. And then you repeat your command.

This may sound harsh. But when you do nothing to curb your child's disobedience, you're rewarding it. Do *not* reward disobedience. The Bible notes a correlation between obeying parents and obeying Christ and all other authorities. Ephesians 5:21 tells us to "submit to one another out of reverence *for Christ*." The Westminster Larger Catechism 124 argues, "By father and mother, in the fifth commandment, are meant not only natural parents, but all superiors in ages and gifts; and especially such as, by God's ordinance, are over us in place of authority, whether in family, church, or commonwealth." Allowing your children to disobey you trains them to disobey God. So staging opportunities isn't cruel. It's loving. It's calmly and clearly developing the character of your child.

ERROR 2
LOW EXPECTATIONS

Finally, remember that first-time obedience isn't just obeying promptly: it's obeying promptly with a pleasant attitude. If your children obey with a bad attitude, they are inwardly rebelling. It's like the little boy who, after his teacher told him to sit down, exclaimed, "I may be sitting down on the outside, but I'm standing up on the inside!" Your children must learn to control not only their actions, but also their attitudes. They must be able to obey instructions without sulking or rolling their eyes.

Make sure you discipline for a bad attitude consistently. If you're inconsistent, then you're just provoking your child to anger. But if you're consistent, you can teach your child to sit down on the inside as well as the outside.

Don't excuse
disobedience.

Parents are very creative with their excuses for disobedience. Here are a few of them.

Some parents will use the excuse of the "strong-willed" child I mentioned before. I don't know who first coined this phrase, but I wish they hadn't. It's an excuse far too many parents use. I don't deny that some children seem to be more compliant than others. But please don't use this excuse for an unruly household. Foolishness is bound up in the heart of a child: every parent has a strong-willed child.

Another excuse is the "Boys!" excuse. Parents of undisciplined boys say, "He's all boy." This is often a way of saying, "He's wild. I can't control him." Indeed, girls do tend to be more compliant than boys. But parents should not have lower standards of obedience for boys than for girls.

You'll hear a lot of parents say, "Every child is unique. You can't raise them all the same way." This is true as far as it goes—but it doesn't mean you can let disobedience slide for some children while cracking down on it for others. I understand that, with some kids, all you have to do is look at them with a suspect eye and they break down crying, while others keep a stiff upper lip and refuse to cry even when you spank them. I get that. But when we say, "Every child is unique. You can't raise them all the same way," I disagree. You do need to raise them the same way—with the same expectations for obedience and respect. Just because you have a son doesn't mean you can excuse his temper tantrums, and just because you have a girl doesn't mean you can allow her to use her (typically) advanced verbal skills to argue with you.

Hopefully the "Every child is unique. You can't raise them all the same way" mantra is pointing to the fact that children have different kinds of gifts. Some are athletic; some are academic. Some like science and math, and others like the humanities. If that's what is meant, then sure, I agree. We shouldn't push an academically gifted child to be the star shortstop, nor should we require the artistic child to be a straight-A student in physics. Just don't use the "Every child is unique. You can't raise them all the same way" phrase to excuse disobedience.

Finally, don't use the "just won't" excuse. You should never hear yourself say, "Johnny just won't take a bath" or, "Johnny just won't come when I call him." If your child won't do something that you command him to do, you've not trained him to obey.

ERROR 2
LOW EXPECTATIONS

Why do we allow disobedience and disrespect? Sometimes it's because disobedience seems pretty harmless in the moment. Sometimes it's because disobedience seems a little cute, especially when it's a small child. Sometimes it's because correcting disobedience simply takes more effort than letting it slide.

Maybe the biggest reason we allow disobedience is because we parents are consumed with ourselves: our social media account, our text message conversation, our documentary on the TV, our nap, etc. Often, I've been in a conversation with a parent, and their child was near them but running wild, and the mom or dad was completely oblivious. They were more interested in our conversation than in training their child. Listen, I can wait—but training your children can't wait. Your social media feed can wait, but your child's disobedience can't. You must quit being selfish and pay attention to the training of your children. I know one mom who left a store without getting anything on her list to deal with her child's behavior. Now that's good parenting! That's putting the training of your children above your own personal needs and desires. Plus, the added benefit is that the children learn Mom is willing to leave a store to discipline them, and therefore, they are more likely to obey.

You have to start requiring first-time obedience early. When your kids are small, issues tend to be

ERROR 2
LOW EXPECTATIONS

somewhat clear. You say things like "Yes," "No," "Stop doing that," and "Put that down." But as they get older, the issues become gray rather than black and white; their sins get bigger, uglier, more complicated. There's an old saying about not being able to teach old dogs new tricks. The training we get when we're young sticks around throughout our lives. Train up a child in the way he should go, and when he is old he will not depart from it.

ACTION 11

Expect your children to control their emotions.

Your child's moods and emotions are not outside the realm of your training. They are manageable. They can be corralled. Every part of your child's personality needs to come under the control of the Lord Jesus Christ. And God has placed you as the parent in the prime spot to help them grow and mature. In the same way that you must train your children to obey and be respectful, you must train them to control their emotions.

Don't let your children be victims of their own moods. One family I know uses the phrase *Think right, act right, feel right*. The mind, being renewed by the Word of God, leads and guides the will. Then the will can choose to obey even when it doesn't feel like it. Finally, emotions follow, like a caboose pulled along by the mind and the will.

Our second-born daughter, Tabby, used to lack confidence. She would rarely try something new or stick her neck out. Whenever we heard about a camp or an activity that we thought would be good for her, she would say that she couldn't do it, that she wouldn't fit in, or some other excuse. And we believed her. One summer, though, we forced her to go to a Christian worldview camp. It was an academic setting, and she didn't know anyone going. Turns out she loved it, "fit in," and thought it was the greatest thing since sliced bread. After that, we always pushed her to get past her initial reluctance and attempt new or interesting things that were out of her comfort zone. Now an adult, she has confidence in spades. Matter of fact, one friend of mine who knows Tabby well refers to her as "Miss Birmingham" because she seems to know and socialize with everyone in town.

Our oldest son, Charlie (older by seven minutes—he's a twin), used to get "bedhead" in a major way. Everyone wakes up with their hair looking bad. It's a part of life. But Charlie was especially prone to some interesting early morning looks. His siblings would make fun of his hair at the breakfast table, and Charlie would start to cry. Lisa and I decided that, rather than trying to get the other four kids to take it easy on the little guy, we would work on Charlie. So we talked to him about how it's not a big deal to have bedhead. We talked about how in life people are always going to be critical or making fun. We showed him a way to respond to their ribbing: just laugh at himself too, and then exaggerate the situation by making his hair even worse. Now Charlie is very secure and unaffected by little things like this. One time not too long afterward his sister told him at the dinner table that he had some dark green lettuce stuck in his tooth that was obvious when he smiled. So what did he do? He looked for the biggest piece of lettuce in his salad and stuck it to his tooth and spent the next five minutes grinning at everybody. You *can* help your children get control of their emotions.

ACTION

Expect to train your children.

Children need to be trained. They are not "plug and play" creatures. Just as a new employee needs to be trained when he starts a new job, children need instruction and guidance in how to behave. Remember: "Folly is bound up in the heart of a child." They need training in obedience, social competence, overcoming pickiness in eating, learning to drive a manual transmission, showing respect, bravery . . . you name it, they need training in it. If training children were not required (in other words, if you could simply let them grow up and they'd be naturally obedient and respectful), we wouldn't be told by the Lord to bring them up in discipline and instruction. Training comes with the territory.

Not many parents realized they were signing up for this sort of task when they had children. It can certainly be overwhelming. But remember three things.

One, training children is a marathon, not a sprint. You will see some good results immediately.

But you will also see children revert back to disobedience. You must train them daily, for weeks, months, and years. Just like diligently exercising will eventually result in bigger muscles and weight loss, diligently training children will eventually produce enjoyable children. So, don't panic if your training seems to take a while before there is an apparent permanent change in their character.

Two, remember that the hard work of training pays off handsomely. Obedient and respectful children are a joy to be around. And it only gets better as they get older and become more like friends and companions.

Three, remember that the Holy Spirit will enable you to do this work. If you look to your own strength, you will not feel up to the task. But the Holy Spirit unites us to Christ, and enables us to bear much fruit as we abide in him (John 15:5). You can do all things through Christ, who strengthens you (Phil. 4:13).

You ought to view parenting like it's boot camp, and you're the drill sergeant. Parenting is not a vacation at the beach where you're left alone to take a nap. Yes, it is an intrusion into your comfort and privacy. And yes, it is an opportunity to help your child become a joyful, godly adult.

Always be looking for chances to train. Firemen practice fighting fires by actually burning down a building in a controlled setting and putting out the fire. Afterward, they debrief and talk about what they did correctly and what they did poorly. Treat life with your children the same way. Stay on the lookout for training opportunities. As a simple example, don't take the "do not touch" items off the coffee table and put them away (except treasured family heirlooms, of course). Rather, keep them there as training opportunities for your child to learn self-control.

One thing we did with our kids was practice speaking to others, because we wanted to work on mumbling and shyness. We would pretend that I was the plumber coming to the house. I would go outside, come to the front door, and ring the doorbell, and we would have one of the kids—one who needed extra training in this matter of mumbling and shyness—answer the door. They were supposed to greet me like I was the plumber and tell me, "Wait just a minute while I go get my mom." If they didn't greet me confidently and with clarity of speech, I went back outside, and we tried it again. Lisa would pretend to be an elderly person at church, and we had the children approach her and initiate a conversation. I would teach my boys how to make eye contact and shake hands firmly: we practiced it at home over and over again.

I remember one time, one of our girls was afraid of going to the dentist. So we set up the living room like it was a dentist's office. Lisa was the hygienist. She came in from another room and called our daughter's name. Lisa took her back into a bedroom, laid her down on the bed, and tapped around on her teeth with an instrument of some sort. Then she told her to wait there for a few minutes. After a few minutes, I came in as the doctor. I introduced myself, talked with her for a moment, and then made her open her mouth, and I tapped around for a few moments more. It was very helpful for our daughter.

You can practice just about anything. Practice going to Walmart. Go out to the car, and drive around the block. Pull back into the driveway (pretending it's the parking lot). Give your kids instructions about how to behave in "Walmart" (your house). Then go inside and pretend you are shopping. If your kids get wild, discipline them. Then take them outside, get in the car, and do it all over again. They'll get the picture. They'll learn how to control themselves. But this takes time. It means you have to view parenting as a job.

One of the most important things you can do is practice sitting quietly in church. This has a double benefit. It gives you the opportunity to develop the character trait of self-control in your child. And it pays practical dividends by allowing you to enjoy worship without constant distraction. Set up the living room as a sanctuary, and have someone be the preacher. Sing some songs, say some long prayers, and read some long passages of Scripture. If your children make small noises or whispers, no big deal. But if they get extra fidgety or will not be quiet, you can discipline them right then and there. Again, this takes time. But the result is children who are enjoyed by both adults and peers alike.

Many parents shudder at the thought that parenting might require this level of obligation and commitment. I remember hearing about a group of ladies in one of my former churches who ate lunch together regularly and called themselves the "Freedom Lunch Club." The way to become a member of the club was to get your last kid sent off to school. The mindset was, "I'm finally free! No more having the shackles of child training to hold me back from doing what I really want to do." This is not the mindset you want to adopt. The Bible says that children are a blessing from the Lord (Ps. 127:3). We should not wish away the years. Does Mom need a break at times? Absolutely. But when parents see their children as interruptions to their lives, it's a problem. Children are one of God's wonderful gifts to remove selfishness and get our eyes off of ourselves.

Indulge me for one last little soapbox speech. To train your children well, you may need a less cluttered life. Training your children probably requires more quiet time at home and less time spent flitting about town, talking on the phone, surfing the web, going to soccer practice, etc. None of these things are bad in and of themselves, but keep in mind that often the good can be the enemy of the best. Paying attention to your children and seeing every moment as a training opportunity will help you to enjoy your children. It will produce children who are obedient and respectful.

ERROR 2
LOW EXPECTATIONS

ACTION 13

Expect to enjoy your children.

Friend, having children should be an incredibly fun, rich, and rewarding experience. My eighteen-year-old self would have never guessed that I would count training children as some of the most rewarding times in my life. Matter of fact, my twenty-seven-year-old-with-two-very-young-children self wouldn't have believed that I would one day have five sons and daughters who love the Lord and are some of my closest friends. When you're in the middle of daily diaper-changing, feeding, and training, you're exhausted. But the richness that children add to your life is hard to overstate. I don't just mean that if you grin and bear it they will one day mature, and you'll enjoy them. I mean that two-year-olds and ten-year-olds and teenagers can be a delight. It's possible to have more laughter in your home when your children are small than you could have ever imagined. It's possible to have more great memories than you could have ever dreamed.

If you don't yet have kids, don't let parents of unruly households sigh and roll their eyes and make you dread being a parent. If you already have kids, rid yourself of the attitude that they are going to be unmanageable and must be endured. You should enjoy being around your children. You should be excited about them being around other people. Well-trained children are a joy wherever they are, both for you and for everyone else.

ERROR

A Child-Centered Home

t would never work on the football field to have a defensive tackle line up as quarterback. Defensive tackles are big and powerful. Quarterbacks are nimble and quick. The right people need to be in the right position. In the same way, there are certain positions that need to be understood and properly manned when it comes to training children.

The most common error in parenting is having a child occupy the central position of the home. You will ruin your children if you center your life around them. They are not designed to be the kings and rulers of the household. They must not think their schedule is the priority schedule in the home. They must not think their activities are the priority activities in the home. You must not walk on eggshells around them and lead them to believe their feelings are the priority feelings in the home.

I've already talked about how parents need to maintain authority, put their marriage first, and put Christ above all. But there are still a variety of subtle ways we can let our children take the quarterback position. I want to cover those here.

Watch what you say.

We need to look at the ways our words communicate, through subtle and not-so subtle means, that the child is the center of the universe.

One way we do this is by asking *okay?* at the end of our sentences. When you tell your child to do something and then say *okay?* as a follow-up, you haven't issued a command—you've asked for permission. Do not ask for permission from your three-year-old. Kids get told what is going to happen; they do not authorize what is going to happen. Either issue a command or do not. But don't issue a command and then ask for your children to authorize it. They are not your judge and jury. You are not accountable to them. (Of course, it isn't wrong to ask your children their opinion about things. Just do not ask their opinion when you are giving commands. Ask their opinion when you sincerely want to know what they think or feel about something.)

Another way we put our children in charge is by asking them *if* they can do something. Say an acquaintance walks up to you at the grocery store, and your child is old enough to say hi. Do not ask him *if* he can say hi to Mr. Brock. What happens when he doesn't say hi? What do you do when he buries his head into your shoulder? Is he disobeying, or not? Either give your children a command and be prepared to follow it up with consequences for disobedience or don't command them to do anything at all.

Along these lines, don't always say, "Thank you" when your child obeys. In Luke 17, Jesus says this:

> "Will any one of you who has a servant plowing or keeping sheep say to him when he has come in from the field, 'Come at once and recline at table'? Will he not rather say to him, 'Prepare supper for me, and dress properly, and serve me while I eat and drink, and afterward you will eat and drink'? Does he thank the servant because he did what was commanded? So you also, when you have done all that you were commanded, say, 'We are unworthy servants; we have only done what was our duty.'" (Luke 17:7–10)

These verses indicate that, when someone obeys his authority, he is simply doing what is proper and expected. When you don't always thank your child for being obedient, you help him, subconsciously, remember that he is not the authority figure or the one who gives orders. He receives orders, and is

ERROR 3
A CHILD-CENTERED HOME

expected to obey them. This sort of mindset helps him submit to other authorities in his life, especially his ultimate authority, God. So don't make a habit of thanking your children when they obey.

Notice what I am saying here: don't *make a habit* of thanking your children when they obey. Certainly thank them at times, especially when they are older and can appreciate you acknowledging their obedience, and when you have asked them to do you a favor ("Please run next door and pick up an egg from Mrs. Jones—she's expecting you"). You can thank them when they do something good without you asking them to do it. It's also a good idea to thank them when you put them to bed and have some time to talk. Tell them how much you appreciate their obedience; tell them what a joy they are; tell them how proud you are of their good attitude. Just don't thank them at the time they are obeying. Obedience is to be expected. When you tell your four-year-old son not to push his sister, he shouldn't be thanked for obeying you.

Don't allow your children to interrupt. There's an old saying that "Children should be seen and not heard." While I'm not necessarily advocating that position, there is a kernel of truth in it. Typically, children rush into a living room where adults are having a conversation and immediately begin talking or asking questions. When you interrupt your conversation to give your child the attention he's demanding, you're teaching him that whatever he has to say is the most important thing in the world. Don't do that. Don't allow your kids to burst into a room and burst forth with a flow of words, demands, or complaints. Instead, teach them the "interrupt rule."

The interrupt rule works like this. Your child wants to say something, but you're in the middle of some sort of conversation. He should quietly walk up to you, place his hand on your leg, shoulder, or forearm, and leave it there until you get an opportunity to address him. It's a good idea for you to place your hand on his hand (while you continue talking to your neighbor), so he knows that you are aware he wants your attention.

Don't continue your conversation with your neighbor for an extended period of time. Probably within thirty seconds or so, you'll be at a place in the conversation where you can pause. But in the meantime, don't allow your child to tug up and down on your sleeve or pant leg. That sort of behavior means he is still demanding your attention, which defeats the purpose of the interrupt rule. I believe it was the Ezzos who said that your child needs to know he shares the world with other people. The interrupt rule is a gesture of honor and respect.

A child should never tell a parent no. If your child tells you no, you have a severe situation on your hands. Swift discipline must follow. Do not talk to him about it. Don't explain things. Just quickly administer discipline. Then tell him, "You don't tell me no." If he keeps it up, discipline him again. And again. And again, if necessary.

Along the same lines, a child should never tell you to wait, or ask you why. Whether he wants to explain his reasoning, or wants you to explain yours, the reality is that he's not obeying. There should never be any questioning of your commands.

No, *wait*, and *why* are the responses of a child who doesn't appreciate authority. If you spend your time explaining things to your children, trying to convince them that a certain course of action is a good one, you're putting them in the place of authority, like a judge who looks at the evidence, hears the arguments, and makes a decision. Your home is not a courtroom. Don't say "your honor" to a child who tries to act like a judge.

Finally, don't allow your children to talk too much. They should not be constantly demanding that you listen to them and answer their questions. Most kids behave like the world exists to hear them speak. We have to combat this. One thing you can do is set a timer and make them play without talking until the timer goes off. The goal is to teach them verbal self-control, and that Mom and Dad don't exist to stay verbally engaged with them.

15

Watch what you give.

Don't overindulge your children. Make them work to earn money for the things they want. Make them pay for stuff themselves. There are several reasons for this. First, constantly giving things to your children builds in them the idea that everything they could want should be provided for them by someone else. This deepens a mindset of "the world revolves around me" that you must extract. Second, children need to learn the value of hard work. If your children never have to go without, they'll never have to learn to take responsibility for their lives. If they don't work hard and wait patiently for their rewards, they will grow up thinking everything will be provided for them on a silver platter. (This advice is especially needed for wealthy families.) Third, making children pay for things themselves teaches them the value of a dollar. When it's their money they are spending, they will think about whether or not they really need what they're asking for.

When our oldest two girls were young teens, they wanted a cell phone. We decided that they would have to pay for the phone and its associated monthly fees through babysitting and other work opportunities. We wanted them to learn that you don't get things handed to you simply because other people have those things. Just because something is "trending" doesn't mean parents should ensure their children are in step with the trend. Especially when it's not a need but rather just a want, children need to think long and hard about whether the cost of the thing is worth the time spent working to afford it.

Christmas and birthdays are other times when you can teach your children that the world does not revolve around them. Some wise parents refuse to give their children everything on their "wish list." Other parents will tell their children to write down only a certain number of items that they want for Christmas or a birthday.

We also need to limit giving our children our undivided attention. Some parents seem to think they must drop everything to accommodate their kids or keep them from being upset. But this teaches them that they rule the roost. Children must learn to play by themselves, without Mom or Dad hovering nearby or being their playmate. By constantly entertaining your kids, you're failing to teach them to think independently, to be comfortable with solitude and quiet, to be content with ordinary and common activities. You're training them to expect life to be a fun-filled circus twenty-four hours a day, seven days a week, where you keep going from one activity to another and one vacation to another and one event to another.

So don't drop everything to fulfill your kids' request, "Come play with me." And don't keep your kids plopped in front of the television or keep their hands filled with a smartphone game, which is another way of making the same mistake. Help your kids learn to entertain themselves.

Remember what I said in the first paragraph here: don't *overindulge* your children. Do, at times, indulge them—especially at Christmas and for birthdays. Give them gifts. Give them yourself. Give them nice things. Life itself is a gift from the Lord, and he showers grace upon abundant grace on a daily basis. Just be sure to make your kids work for things too. Don't overdo it when it comes to gift-giving.

ACTION

16

Say no.

We put our children in the driver's seat when we don't tell them no.

One occasion in particular where we put our children in the driver's seat is at mealtimes. We give in to our children by allowing them to control what they eat. For example, if your child won't eat anything but chicken fingers and therefore you only eat at the local chicken tenders place, then you have a child-centered home. If Mom becomes a short-order cook because "Joey doesn't like tomatoes" and "Suzie only eats macaroni and cheese these days," then you have a child-centered home. This will be particularly embarrassing to you when you are eating at a friend's house and your child exclaims, "Gross. I don't like that."

I remember several times dealing with one of our kids (Bryant, the other twin) who would not eat his supper when he was about five years old, particularly the vegetables and salad. Whenever this happened, we would let him leave the table and go play—but he wouldn't get anything but water the rest of the night. In the morning, we would pull his plate out of the refrigerator (covered with cling wrap), warm it up, and put it in front of him. Once again, he would pass. So we would put him down, and he'd go play. Nothing to eat and nothing to drink but water until lunch (unless he said he wanted the uneaten food mid-morning—we'd let him eat that). Then lunch would come around, and we'd repeat the same thing: pull his plate out of the refrigerator, warm it up, and put it in front of him. Yet again, he'd pass, and yet again, nothing to eat and drink but water. By the time three o'clock or so rolled around, Bryant would be lethargic and looking pale and pathetic. It was a sad sight. If he were our first-born, we might have been a little nervous about his health. But because he was number five, we knew he would be just fine. At this point, usually one of his more merciful older sisters (Tabby) would be pleading with him to eat. Finally, he'd ask for the food, and we'd once again pull his plate out of the refrigerator (still covered with cling wrap), warm it up, and put it in front of him. This time, after about twenty-four hours without food, he'd eat. Today Bryant eats his vegetables and salads without complaint! And, more importantly, he knows that the world doesn't revolve around him.

There are other ways to fight the mealtime battle. You can make your picky eater eat half of their supper. You can assign a certain number of bites (with parental approval of the bite size!). However, don't coax or bribe a child to eat. Don't play the "Open up, here comes the choo choo train!" game. Simply put the food before them. When you plead and play games, all adult conversation comes to a close, and the child is now the center of attention at the table. Remember, the goal is to teach your children that they are not the center of the universe.

In addition to giving in to our children at mealtimes, another way we give in to our children is by allowing them to disobey. I touched on this before. Whenever they "win" and get away with disobedience, it strengthens their resolve to disobey next time. They know that if they are determined enough, they will get what they want. Don't train your child to treat the world with a "my way or the highway" mentality.

Let me give you a good example of not giving in. One time we were visiting our friends for dinner. The kids had spent the evening learning magic tricks and occasionally running in to perform them for the adults. When it was time for us to leave, their daughter Esther started crying because she hadn't had a chance to do her magic trick. Probably it would have been fine for us to stay another few minutes. But her parents told her no and that the Brocks needed to leave. So we went on our way. Esther was not happy and began to cry and pout. The Burtons didn't stop us and ask us to stay so she could do her trick. They didn't intervene for her by asking us to change our plans. They didn't give in to her whining.

Esther learned a lot that night. By not giving in, her parents taught her that her desires don't dictate how everyone else lives. She learned that manipulation, especially tears, do not get you what you want. These are amazing lessons that your kids need to learn early. This is training the heart.

Many adults get angry with the fact that they don't get everything they want in life. Maybe it's called a mid-life crisis, depression, or bitterness. If you're careful not to give in to your children when they are young, you're preparing them to be less susceptible to anger when they don't get their way in the future.

Never allow your children to boss you around. This is one of the biggest no-no's of parenting. You give the orders, not them. The Ezzos use the "red cup/blue cup" example to illustrate this. When your child asks for something to drink, what may happen is that you pull down the red sippy cup, and your child asks for the blue sippy cup instead. If you acquiesce to his request, you are, in a very subtle way, communicating to him that he can boss you around and have what he wants. Many parents are wise enough not to give in if the kid is hysterical about having the blue cup, crying and begging and so forth. But even if your child politely asks for a certain color cup, saying no to his request is a good opportunity for the compliant, easy-going child to learn that life doesn't always give you what you want.

It's not the end of the world to *occasionally* say, "You can have the blue cup." Or maybe you could ask them beforehand which color cup they want. But this needs to be *rare*, not regular. Our children need to see clearly that the world doesn't revolve around them. One of the best ways to communicate that is by not giving in to their requests. Say no often! And the younger your child is when you start saying no, the better.

Make sure to tell your kids no pleasantly. Don't be grumpy when you announce that it's time to leave the cousins' house. Have a pleasant demeanor and a soft tone to your voice when you give commands. You ought to be able to do that. If they disobey, simply discipline them. Remember, if you discipline immediately, you won't get angry.

One of the great benefits of this type of parenting is that it develops children who are really rather enjoyable to be around. The fact is most people don't enjoy having kids around because they're brats; they're whiny and disrespectful and full of bad attitude. But kids who are obedient, respectful, and not demanding are a joy. Adults are glad to visit with them.

Bottom line: having a child-centered home is likely idolatry. You spend every day sacrificing to your little demanding and moody gods. To quote the Ezzos: "When a child's happiness is a greater goal than his holiness, when his psychological health is elevated above moral health, and when he, not God, becomes the center of the family universe, a subtle form of idolatry is created. Children become little gods who have parents worshiping their creation and not their Creator."[1] As we read in 1 John 5:21, keep yourselves from idols.

---

1. Gary and Anne Marie Ezzo, *Growing Kids God's Way: Reaching the Heart of Your Child with a God-Centered Purpose*, 5th ed. (Simi Valley, CA: Growing Families International, 1998), 48.

Say yes.

While you should tell your children no often and early, as they get older, tell them yes as much as possible! Don't be the parent with a constantly furrowed brow who never seems to enjoy life. Your kids want to sleep outside in the doghouse with the dog? Sure, go ahead. Your daughter wants to wear the same shirt four days in a row? Okay. Your son wants to try fencing instead of soccer? Go for it. As they mature, say yes often. Show them that you're not afraid, unhappy, or anxious. Show them that you're secure and pleasant. Help them make memories. Allow them to try things and fail. A Christ-centered home is full of joy, grace, and freedom.

Children need to be free to try things and fail. Children need to be free to walk to the park and back by themselves. Children need to feel free to skip school (with parental permission) to go to the afternoon Braves game. Children need to learn to play with fire (in a bonfire sort of way) and pocketknives. In many, many ways our children need freedom. So, give it to them. Don't be a helicopter parent always saying no and refusing to let them out of your sight.

I opened this chapter by saying that parents must occupy the proper position in the home. What I'm saying here is that parents must also *change* "positions" at different stages in a child's life. How you train your children will evolve over time. I can't recall where I first heard it, but I've found the following taxonomy to be helpful:

Until age 6, you are a "cop" to your child. These are the days of strict discipline and accountability.

From ages 6 to 12, you are a "coach" to your child. As a coach you will continue to discipline them, but there will be much more conversation, with both correction and affirmation.

From ages 12 to 18, you become more like a "counselor" to your child. As a counselor you'll listen to them; you'll try to guide them through rough times. Counselors help others to see God's hand in their lives and to know the difference between good things and better things, or between acceptable things and wiser things. Counselors ask questions more than simply giving answers. This allows your child to learn to think through things for themselves.

After age 18, you become more like a "companion friend" to your child. Friends still challenge each other and "call out" sin in each other's lives. But they also simply spend time together, share the same values, and build up each other in their faith. This is the end goal of your parental training. It's a joy to have a child who is a friend and companion.

If you don't go through this progression I've noted above and, in a sense, "let up" on your children as they get older, you will frustrate them, anger them, and embitter them against you. Remember: be strict on your children when they're small, so you can lighten up when they're tall. No adult likes being treated like a toddler. Treat your children according to their age.

ERROR

4

Failing to Discipline

We neglect things we don't value. We guard the things we do. When you neglect to discipline your children, you're teaching them that the Bible's standards and values are unimportant—they aren't worth guarding. But when you discipline your children regularly, you're teaching them that those standards and values mean something, that they will be protected and treasured. Think about how you treat a paper plate compared to your grandmother's ceramic dishware: the one that is more precious to you gets more attention and care.

Discipline is necessary. Tenderhearted parents need to be very diligent to stand firm in their efforts to correct their children. It's easy to let your emotions get the best of you and relax your standards, especially when your child seems sorrowful and apologetic. But you must stay the course. Don't be more merciful than God. Since the Lord disciplines those he loves (Heb. 12:6), imitating him means disciplining your kids. Don't think you're being loving when you neglect your children's discipline.

ACTION 18

Fit the punishment to the crime.

When it comes to discipline for bad behaviors, the punishment must fit the crime. This is what the Bible means when it talks about an "eye for an eye" (Lev. 24:19–21). This means that some discipline of our children will consist of lighter bits of chastisement, while at other times our discipline will be more severe. But in all cases it must be just.

Children will disobey us. They will hurt us. But a parent who takes it personally will not seek to discipline in a reciprocal manner, but rather will seek to hurt the child in return. This is why parenting has to begin with parents. You must respond to your child's disobedience maturely.

There are many ways to discipline. While spanking and training swats are the primary tools for discipline (more on that in the following chapters), they are not the only ones. The goal of discipline is simply to encourage obedience and discourage disobedience. Encourage obedience with words of affirmation, goals, rewards, and practice runs (like the living room "dentist trip" I mentioned earlier).

Discourage disobedience with verbal rebukes, natural consequences, time-outs, training swats, and spankings. While many folks would like a flowchart showing when to use each of the above-mentioned tactics, that's just not possible. Training children isn't that easy. It takes lots of prayer, trial and error, conversation, and evaluation. Still, let's go into a little more detail, starting with the positive side of discipline.

You need to be full of affirmation and praise for your children. Encourage good behavior and good attitudes. When you do this, be sure to be specific. Don't just tell your children how happy you are to be their dad. Tell them how happy it makes you when they serve in the church nursery or say no to a job offer that would have required them to miss worship on the Lord's Day. In addition, be sure to mention the character quality that prompted the activity: "You showed a lot of perseverance when you didn't quit the track team, even though it was not very enjoyable for you." Praise them when they do an outstanding job. Praise them when they fail but put in an excellent effort. Praise them in quiet times of conversation, when it's late at night and they're just crawling into bed, or when you go out to lunch one-on-one.

Using incentives when certain goals are reached is a good way to positively instill discipline into your children. Businesses reward salesmen with financial bonuses when they reach their quota for the year. For younger children, you might give them a homemade coupon for ice cream if they complete their Saturday chores before noon. You might give older children a pool party with friends if they make straight A's in school. Teenagers could be given a $100 gift card when they learn to drive a manual transmission car.

Remember, obedience is expected. Use incentives not for obedience, but for the development of skills, talents, and character: things like work ethic, a good mind, and the ability to drive all kinds of vehicles in the future. Encourage your kids to try new things and learn new skills. Charge them to attempt things in which they may likely fail. Reward them for hard work.

On the negative side of discipline, a legitimate tool is verbal reproof. A verbal reproof is when parents simply tell their children that they don't approve of their behavior. One of my girls ran for a cross-country team when she was about twelve years old. She had a habit of getting "cramps" or "stitches" in her side during runs. At one particular meet she passed by trotting very slowly, much slower than her usual pace. After we got home she told me that she was afraid of getting a stitch in her side, and that's why she was not trying very hard. You better believe I verbally reproved her. I was quite disappointed that fear of pain kept her from doing her duty and being a good teammate. Certainly actual pain will limit one's ability to be their best. But acting in fear of what may or may not happen deserved a good tongue-lashing. Verbal reproof can be an appropriate "fit" to various "crimes."

However, this form of discipline should not be used very often in the early years. Verbal reproof simply doesn't work as well when children don't yet have good abstract thinking abilities. Younger children don't mentally connect your words with their behavior. But they do connect their behavior with the pain of a swat. As children mature, they develop the ability to make logical connections between your words of admonition and their behavior. Until that point, verbal reproof is not effective.

Allowing children to suffer the natural consequences of their mistakes and decisions is another way to discipline, especially when a child is not willfully defiant, but simply forgetful or careless. I remember one such occasion with our son Charlie. He had shown interest in the electrical outlets. Lisa and I had told him not to mess with the outlets or put anything into them, but . . . You know where this is going, right? One day we both were in the back of the house, and the lights flickered off and on, and we heard a *tzzzzt* sound. Then about a half second later, we heard Charlie screaming. (Thankfully. When something like that happens and your child *isn't* screaming, it's probably not good.) We ran up to the front of the house, and there was Charlie standing in front of the electrical outlet. A black streak ran up the wall, and it smelled like something was burning. Charlie had crammed some keys into the contact opening. Thankfully, he was not hurt, and there was no fire going on behind the drywall.

Did we spank Charlie? That would seem appropriate, right? He had disobeyed us. But we believed that he had learned his lesson. The natural consequences did the job for us.

Don't rescue your children from the natural consequences of their mistakes. If your child leaves his bike in the yard and it gets wet from rain or dew, don't go pick it up yourself. Make him do it. And if he forgets or is lazy and the chain rusts, make him pay for a new one.

Losing privileges is yet another way to practice what I'm calling negative discipline. Like verbal reproof, this will be more effective with older kids than younger ones. And I'd encourage you to have the loss of privilege relate to the infraction itself. For example, if you have a child who gets to stay up later on Friday night, but he disobeys orders to go to bed early on Thursday, then take away his Friday night privileges. If your child misbehaves with the neighbor kid, have your child lose the privilege of playing with him for a period of time. An example of *not* connecting the loss of privilege with the infraction would be taking away your child's front seat privileges for going over his computer game time limit. Those two aren't really connected. If your child refuses to quit playing on his electronics when you tell him to, he shouldn't lose front seat privileges, he should lose electronics privileges.

The last tool of negative discipline is spanking, which I'll cover in the next chapters on toddlers and grade-schoolers. At this point, you just need to know that you don't have to spank for every infraction. Be creative in your discipline. When God disciplines us, it varies in how he administers it. Your goal is to discipline. And so long as the discipline is painful, and fits the crime, the discipline is effective.

Discipline *is* painful. But pain is a gift from God. In 2 Corinthians 12, Paul writes about his "thorn in the flesh." He writes about how his thorn in the flesh kept him from being proud. That painful thorn was a kind gift from the Lord to Paul. The discipline you inflict upon your child is also a kind gift to them. Don't shun God's methods by trying to rescue your child from going through painful experiences.

Be angry at sin.

Some people believe that you should "never discipline your child when you're angry." This is an overrated modern axiom. Of course, you should always be under control when disciplining your child. You should not attempt to discipline when you are hysterical, or on the verge of abuse. You should never shout at your child (probably the number one sin of mothers). Name-calling and sarcasm equals "out of control." You should never physically harm your child.

But it's perfectly fine for your children to see you angry, so long as that anger is under control and directed at the right thing: sin. A furrowed brow is okay when sin is committed. When I see my kids disrespect Lisa, I'm angry—and they need to know it. I don't have to yell, scream, take off my belt to spank them, and twirl around the room like the Tasmanian Devil. They can tell I'm angry when I'm simply stern and serious.

We live in a world today that values niceness, timidity, and participation trophies. Expressing displeasure to children is frowned upon. Everybody is afraid of saying something that might cause children discomfort. Some parents have taken this idea to the extreme and refuse to discipline their children because "it's not nice." But it's right for you to be angry when you are disobeyed or when an authority figure is disrespected. You and I should be angry at sin—and our kids should see it.

Remember that God disciplines; he is angry at sin. Don't make yourself out to be godlier than God.

If you quickly lose self-control and could possibly get violent—yes, wait until you are cooled off to deal with your child. Send him to his room while you give yourself a "parental time-out" by going to your room and praying. Maybe this would be a good time to call a mentor, explain the situation, and get perspective before implementing discipline (or, perhaps your conversation with your mentor will help you realize that discipline isn't even necessary in this situation). And don't "lose it" over spilled milk throughout the day. You and I should be angry at sin; we shouldn't be angry at traffic. Our kids shouldn't see us yelling at other drivers.

Grow in the Lord and get victory over your anger. If you're disciplining in anger at 4 p.m., it is likely that you *should* have disciplined at 3:50 p.m. In other words, it's really *your fault* that your blood pressure is up and that you're on the verge of disciplining with inappropriate anger. If you put first-time obedience into practice, you'll have fewer opportunities to get angry in the first place.

Be consistent.

Parents must be steady in their discipline. You can't punish disobedience one time and let it go the next. You can't chastise disrespect on Mondays, Wednesdays, and Fridays, but let it go on Tuesdays and Thursdays. Your children won't know what to expect of you. Be consistent.

· This means you must pay attention. You can't be so engrossed in your own world that you miss opportunities to discipline. When it comes to kids, especially younger kids, your TV show, conversation, computer, and phone must be put aside. You will kill any progress you're trying to make if you're distracted and therefore inconsistent. You will exasperate your children.

Often it goes something like this. You ignore your children's minor bad attitudes and disobedience to negligible commands because you are caught up in your own world. When their sin becomes unignorable, you come rumbling to life and bring down the hammer. Then you go back to not paying attention, and your children go back to their poor attitudes and petty disobedience, wondering when you will explode next. This type of inconsistency is exasperating.

ERROR 4
FAILING TO DISCIPLINE

Another extremely common way to exasperate your child is failing to get their attention when giving a command. This is especially important at young ages. Ask the child to look at you. You could even say, "Let me see your eyes." Then give the command. You can also require confirmation that they heard and understood you by having them respond with, "Yes, ma'am." This eliminates many problems, especially the "I didn't hear you" excuse for disobedience. Be sure your children hear you.

There are many gray areas parents have to deal with. Your children's disobedience isn't always black and white. You may wonder if they actually heard your command. You may question whether or not they really crossed the line. Here's a piece of advice: be super consistent on the clear things and don't get too frustrated by the vague things. Sometimes you'll feel unsure about the facts. But don't lose too much sleep over it. Just be consistent every time you know there was disobedience.

21

Subsidize and penalize.

You get more of what you subsidize and less of what you penalize. I first heard this principle from Douglas Wilson. It works in all areas of life. Whatever you give toward, you will get more of. If you are a landlord and allow your tenant to be late with his monthly rent, he will keep being late with his monthly rent. If you penalize him for it, he will start paying on time (or move out, in which case you will get a new tenant).

The same thing is true in training children. If your son won't clean his room, so you do it for him, he will continue to leave his room messy. If your daughter whines and you give her your attention because she's whining, you will get more whining. If you always buy your children new toys because they keep dropping and breaking their old ones, you'll get more drops and carelessness. On the other hand, if your son cleans his room without being told to do it, and you commend him for it, you will get more unprovoked room-cleaning. If you give your children some bonus money for being particularly detailed in the way they washed the windows, you will get more excellence. You get more of what you subsidize and less of what you penalize. This is the basic principle of discipline, really. This is a basic principle for life.

Never do something for your child that you told him to do. Take, for example, the matter of taking out the trash. If you told your child to take out the trash and he forgot, and now it's eleven o'clock at night and he's in bed . . . what do you do? I'd encourage you to wake him up and have him take it out. You don't have to wake him up and yell at him; you don't have to wake him up with your eyes rolling and sarcasm dripping from your lips about his lazy rear end. Simply remind him politely that he was supposed to take out the trash and he forgot, so he needs to get up and do it.

It would only take a few seconds for you to do it yourself, but the goal is not to get the trash down to the street. The goal is to get your child developed and disciplined; the goal is to build character, and taking out the trash is a means to that end.

Think about it. People don't continue to do things when they get punished for them. I don't put my hand on a hot stove element because *it hurts*. It's the same thing with our kids. If they're punished for doing something, they'll eventually quit doing it. But if they're not punished, they'll just keep going. I remember one time that I was a bad example of this. My son Charlie played on the school baseball team. Before one of the games, he sent me a text asking me to bring something that he forgot to pack. Well, Dumb Me brought him his stuff. And so he did it again. And then I brought it to him a second time! What I should have done was tell him no and make him suffer the consequences of not playing in the game because he wasn't in proper uniform. I bet that would have, as we say in the South, "learned him."

Related to this is the truth that the reward or punishment must be greater than the gain from disobedience. I've heard many parents complain that their child continues to disobey even though they discipline him with "grounding." Then I learn that the child was "grounded" but still had access to his phone, computer, and TV. Or parents wonder why their child won't obey "even if I give her an M&M." Parents are competing against the reward for disobedience, and their punishments and rewards must be up to the task.

If you want your children to continue their disobedience, disrespect, whining, laziness, arguing, and fighting, then just give in and let them still get what they want. But if you want those things to stop, you must subsidize their positive efforts and penalize their bad behavior.

ERROR 4

FAILING TO DISCIPLINE

Distinguish "I'm sorry" from "Please forgive me."

"Please forgive me" and "I'm sorry" don't mean the same thing. It's important for your children to understand the difference.

Children will make many mistakes. They'll spill their milk. They'll accidentally hurt someone. They'll carelessly walk through the house and cause damage. It happens. When these sorts of things take place, children should say, "I'm sorry." They say, "I'm sorry" in these situations because it was an accident, not a sin. Therefore children should simply express their sorrow for the episode.

On the other hand, children will, with malice aforethought, spit on other children, pull hair, steal toys, punch, scream, and cause all manner of havoc. When these types of things take place, children shouldn't say, "I'm sorry." They have sinned against someone else, and they need to ask the other person to forgive them. A full way to say it would be something like this: "I was wrong for hitting you, Mommy. I should have obeyed you. Will you please forgive me?"

Some of you may think I'm making a mountain out of a molehill and that it's just a matter of semantics. I disagree. It gets to the heart of the matter. Children need to understand the seriousness of sin and the depravity of their hearts. Asking for forgiveness uses biblical terminology and gets them used to the idea of confessing sin. Yes, they learn about this conceptually when they learn to pray the Lord's Prayer, but in the home they learn to be specific and personal. So don't assume there's no difference between saying, "I'm sorry" and asking for forgiveness.

23

Affirm character, not (just) appearances.

Don't affirm your child's external features over his or her character traits. When you prioritize your children's looks or performance, you teach them to focus on appearances. This makes them insecure. Instead, you should encourage, support, and compliment strong character.

Say your daughter has only heard you compliment her beautiful cheekbones or gorgeous eyes. If she's in a car crash and her face is disfigured, or if she develops a thyroid issue that keeps her from being able to lose weight, her sense of security and identity will be crushed. She'll wonder if she has any value.

The same thing can be said about performance. If all you do is compliment your son's athleticism on the football field, then what happens if he doesn't get a scholarship to college? He's lost. His security was wrapped up in his football skills, but now that it's obvious he's not quite good enough, he'll have to look somewhere else for attention and acceptance. That usually leads down a bad path.

In high school, I knew twin brothers. Both were pretty good athletes, but one was not quite as good as the other. While his brother received a small scholarship to play in college, he didn't get anything. For a while he played as part of the scout team. But knowing he would never see the actual football field on a Saturday, and tired of getting beat up on the scout team, he decided to quit.

When he lost football, he lost everything. This previously disciplined and straightlaced guy began experimenting with drugs. In a few months he was hooked. He became promiscuous and immoral in his relationships with girls. He became the guy who could outdrink everyone at any party.

This kid had grown up in a decent home, and he had walked the straight and narrow for many years. Why did he leave the path of wisdom and pursue a life of sin? I'm convinced that it's in large part because the thing he had always been respected and complimented for—his athletic prowess—was now gone. He was a nobody. Nobody likes being a nobody. So he went searching elsewhere for attention and respect, for acknowledgment that he was still worth noticing.

Compliment character. Tell your pretty daughter what a kind demeanor she has. Praise her for the way she presents herself in a respectable manner. Thank her for always seeking out the "wallflower" and trying to include that lonely person in the group. With your sports-loving son, praise him for his hustle. Compliment his ability to work as a part of a team. Commend him for playing through pain and never quitting.

Your children don't have much say-so in how they look, or whether they have inborn athletic or musical skills or a naturally high IQ. It's certainly fine to notice those gracious gifts from the Lord. Just don't overdo it. What they *do* have control over is their ability to work hard, develop natural talents, express love to others, and show zeal for truth and righteousness. Compliment them for the traits that they can work on and develop.

Allow your children to appeal.

One of the things I've said repeatedly is that your children should promptly respond to your commands with obedience. However, there will be times when your child is confused or genuinely thinks you wouldn't have given the command if you had some additional information. Therefore, it's helpful for parents to train children how to make *appeals*. The Ezzos taught us this little technique.

Let's say the family is spring-cleaning, and Mom is in the back of the house. She tells her son to go to the garage to get some cleaning solution—but on his way to the garage, Dad tells him to go clean his room. The child has been given two commands that contradict each other. What's he supposed to do?

An appeal solves this dilemma. The child asks if he can make an appeal. Dad says he may. Then the child can tell Dad what Mom commanded, and Dad can tell him to go on his way getting the cleaning stuff. Appeals are helpful for when a child receives contradictory instructions and one of his parents is unaware of the situation.

ERROR 4
FAILING TO DISCIPLINE

Appeals are also helpful for situations like when a child is reading a book and Mom tells him to brush his teeth, put on his pajamas, and go to bed. If he is on the last page of the chapter, he should be comfortable enough with his parents' leadership to say, "May I appeal?" After Mom says yes, he can tell her that he only has one page left, and Mom can decide whether to let him finish.

There are a few things to keep in mind here. The appeal process won't ordinarily be helpful for young children. It's too abstract of a concept for the little ones to appreciate or know how to use. You'll have to gauge when your child is old enough to understand it.

In addition, after your child learns how the appeal technique works, they'll be tempted to stretch its meaning and use it to lengthen the time they can make their case, or to pit one parent against another. That's not the purpose. An appeal should only be used when there's some information that a parent doesn't have. And it should only be made to the parent issuing the command.

"But Mom!" and "I can't because . . . " are not appeals. These words spring from a defiant spirit. Repeated appeals are also not really appeals but arguments. An appeal may be made only once. Even when making an appeal, your child's attitude should honor your authority in the home.

Once in a blue moon you might want to say, "No, you may not appeal" to your child's request, simply to keep him from thinking he can manipulate the situation. It's a good thing for your children to be constantly reminded that Mom and Dad are in charge and they are not.

One of the benefits of the appeal technique is that it incentivizes children to obey. Knowing Mom and Dad are reasonable encourages regular obedience. It helps your children trust you, which is very important as they get older. Teenagers especially need to believe that Mom and Dad are approachable and flexible.

It isn't that hard to teach your children how to make an appeal. Put Mom in one room and Dad in another. Have your child get a command from Mom, then have him leave the room to perform the task. Have Dad give a contradictory command. Have your child ask, "May I appeal?" Then Dad should negate his command in some way, and your child can see how fun it is to obey and communicate maturely with reasonable parents.

ACTION 25

Build memories.

One of the best things you can do as a parent is build memories with your children. Fun memories are a constant encouragement: families that have a lot of "Remember when . . ." conversations are always laughing together. Difficult times bind families together, and their memory can remind them of their shared values. Memory is a wonderful gift from the Lord that gives us a sense of history and connection with others.

It's easy to build memories, really. Two of the best ways to do it are by doing something new, and by doing something over and over again.

When you repeat activities as a family, you're creating traditions and shaping hearts. Anything you do repeatedly shapes the heart. So even if you are tired of watching *It's a Wonderful Life* every Christmas Eve, keep at it. Traditions root us in families and places. They help your children feel grounded and stable.

Some families take a camping trip every year. Some families go on a mission trip every year. We Brocks always went to the exact same spot for vacation with the same friends. Laughter erupts when we talk about the time a bat flew into the house, the men were shocked by a snake in the boathouse, or the kids were thrown off the tube while being pulled by the boat. At home, we had family cooking competitions, went on "dessert runs," and watched and played lots and lots of baseball. Now that the boys are older, we play golf together and compete for the Brock family trophy. It's hard to overestimate the value of repeated activities and how they have a stabilizing effect on us.

The other way to build memories is to try something you've never done before. The great thing about trying something new is that you'll build a memory no matter how it goes: it can be a great success, or it can be a total failure, and it will still create a lasting memory.

One time a Krispy Kreme Doughnuts was opening up in our hometown. They were going to give out free doughnuts and T-shirts to the first one hundred people who came through the doors—so a few nights before it opened, the local college students started camping out in the parking lot. My kids (ages six to fourteen at the time) wanted to camp out too. So we said, "Let's go for it." We got a couple of other kids from the church, loaded up a fifteen-passenger van, and headed off to Krispy Kreme. That night a cold front came through, and by the time the store opened in the morning, it was freezing. We slept in the van. We had to drive several times during the night to a local gas station for the kids to use the bathroom. When it was finally five in the morning, the kids got in line. One thing we often laugh about was how Priscilla got squished by a fat man in the pushing and shoving to be one of the first hundred people in the door (she was holding the door open, and the crowd behind the fat man pushed him into her). We came home with our free doughnuts, free T-shirts, and lots of fun memories.

Even though creating memories may not be too difficult, it isn't always cheap. Going on vacations, buying bikes so you can ride them together around the neighborhood, going to Alabama football games . . . memories can be costly. But love is not stingy, and the payoff is worth it. Invest in your family by building memories.

INTERLUDE

It Isn't Too Late

Throughout the remainder of this book, I will be addressing how to deal with issues that apply to children at specific ages. But before we continue, I want to address any feelings of guilt you may have for the way you have trained your children. Maybe you're reading this and you feel like you've made too many mistakes. Perhaps you think there's too much water under the bridge. Maybe you wonder if your kids are too old to start correcting them. What do you do? Is there a way to recover lost ground? I believe there is. The Bible gives us good instruction here. Proverbs 28:13 reads, "Whoever conceals his transgressions will not prosper, but he who confesses and forsakes them will obtain mercy." This teaches us how to begin recovering lost ground: admit our mistakes.

Christians should be characterized by confession of sin. Do that! Confess your failures to the Lord and to your children. Tell your kids that things are going to be different from now on. Ask for their forgiveness for whatever specific parenting failures you are convicted of by the Holy Spirit.

One tremendous benefit of "pressing the reset button" like this is that your kids learn what humility looks like. They learn that it's okay to admit mistakes. I remember hearing a child say about her dad, "Oh, he'd never admit he was wrong." What a terrible thing for a child to think! The essence of Christianity is admitting your need for a Savior. When you fail to admit your sins, you teach your children never to admit their sins. You teach them that they don't need Jesus. But when you do admit your sins to your children, you model humility and repentance. You show them how to rely on Christ, not on your own righteousness.

As you improve your parenting, make sure to communicate with gentleness. Don't show up at home with the posture of "There's a new sheriff in town." Be gentle. It has probably taken you some time to develop your new paradigm for training children, so be patient with them as they adapt to this new parent in their home. Your children will appreciate tenderness and kindness.

Also, when you begin to make changes in the way you train your children, know that you will encounter resistance. Children are sinners. Keep this in mind. Previously, you were permissive or disengaged, and your children were able to do whatever they wanted. But as an engaged, non-permissive parent, you will be resisting the children's ability to do whatever they want. The more involved you get in the training of your children, the more sparks will fly. If you remember that they are sinners just like you, you won't be surprised by this.

This points to something we've talked about before: the real key to parenting is the gospel.

This means you, as a parent, recognize how sinful you are. It means you recognize how difficult it is to obey. It means you are humble. You are patient. You know your children need a heart change, just like you. If you aren't comfortable with the concept of forgiveness, you'll have a hard time turning your home around. But when you know the good news of Jesus, you know that you're loved, accepted, and adopted into the family of God. You're free to admit your sin, thank God for forgiveness and the righteousness of Christ, and move on. And you can help your children do the same thing.

Being humble, secure in Christ, and transparent about your sin results in happier and holier homes. When you're able to be honest about your sin, you become lighthearted and joyful, rather than exhausted from trying to keep up a charade of your own righteousness. You honor and obey the Lord out of gratitude, which results in a broad and deep obedience rather than a cursory change. The gospel of Jesus is the foundation for making any progress in recovering lost ground, whether in your own life or in the lives of your children.

Remember: God is sovereign. He is always at work in our children's lives, even when we have not trained them well. Every parent has failures. But God works through our mistakes. Salvation and sanctification are his responsibility, and no one, not even a bad parent, can thwart his will. Parents are responsible to do their best with the light they have every moment of every day, and then trust the results to the Lord.

ERROR

Reasoning with
Your Toddler

I t's one of the funnier things I see: a parent going into great detail explaining to their two-year-old why it's not proper to hit Mommy in the face. Of course, hitting Mommy in the face is a bad thing. But the problem is that some parents think their toddler (nine months to three years old) can understand abstract concepts like love and respect and will think about those things before they misbehave. No matter how smart your toddler is, when you plead with him not to hurt Mommy, he's not tracking with you. There will be plenty of time to do some explaining when your kids get a little older (see upcoming chapters). But trying to get your toddler to make logical connections between abstract concepts is a waste of your breath.

What's needed in the toddler years is lots of spanking, not talking. Toddlers need only to associate their misbehavior with your "No" and the pain of a swat. A couple years of this, and your child will become self-controlled and enjoyable. (Frankly, if you discipline consistently from age nine months to eighteen months, most of the work will be already done.) On the other hand, if you spend these toddler years just trying to get them to understand *why* they shouldn't spit on their brother, smack you in the face, or whine incessantly, you'll still be talking to them when they're teenagers, because they never learned any self-control.

Use training swats.

In this section we finally turn to the subject of spankings. Earlier I noted that there are two types of spankings that you can employ: training swats and traditional spankings. This section will focus primarily on training swats, which are essentially spankings but more immediate (you administer the swat without going away to a private spot) and less forceful (it's only a slight sting versus a more intense pain). Training swats are most useful for toddlers, when the goal of discipline is simply to associate disobedience with pain.

I call this kind of spanking "training swats" because your mindset at this point should be very much in the mode of a trainer. You've adopted the point of view of a drill sergeant, out to produce a disciplined, self-controlled marine. You don't try to avoid disciplining your children. You look for opportunities to correct them, all day, every day. And when you give your fifteen-month-old a command, you have your switch in hand, ready to swat. The toddler years are a brief window where your children are still very moldable. Use those years to train them in obedience and self-control.

I mentioned looking for opportunities to train your child. The mindset I'm encouraging here is to think to oneself, "I ought to go into the living room and interrupt his playing with his toys and tell him, 'Come here.'" The whole purpose of the command is not because you really need him to come to you but because you have the attitude of a trainer. Again, using training swats is more of a mindset than a radically different way of spanking.

As I said, training swats should begin when your child is around nine months old. Prior to this age, kids don't have much ability to express their defiance to your commands and instructions. You probably won't be giving many commands or instructions anyway, because *you know* they can't fulfill them. But as they get closer to becoming toddlers, they gain the ability to understand and obey—or not.

Toddlers need constant correction, without much conversation. They need frequent discipline that is immediately applied, so that the punishment is clearly connected to the crime. As a result, spanking at this stage is the better option over time-outs, loss of privilege, and natural consequences. If you spank your children with training swats regularly and consistently, you will not experience the "terrible twos." You won't have temper tantrums thrown at Walmart.

When your child is very young, I suggest swatting the back of his leg if he's whining or squirming and using your hand to smack the top of his hand if he's touching something he shouldn't. As he gets a little older, swat him on the buttocks or, if he's wearing a diaper, just below the diaper on the back of the upper thigh. Spanking should never be on the back, face, arms, or torso.

You can use a variety of instruments for these training swats. But I suggest using a flexible rod of some sort, like a switch, a wooden spoon, or a thin dowel rod. These have the great ability to sting yet not bruise. Lisa and I used different types of switches through the years. The best tool we ended up finding was, strangely enough, a polybutylene supply line from the plumbing department. This is a plastic, flexible rod that we would purchase at about eighteen inches in length. At least once I remember getting a six-foot piece and cutting it into multiple eighteen-inch strips to have around the house. We would put them in multiple places so that one would always be readily at hand, easy to find.

I discuss spanking grade-schoolers in detail in the next chapter. There I describe a process that includes finding a private spot, having a conversation, praying together, etc. Training swats have none of that. Training swats are immediate, a swift response to disobedience.

Let's take an example. Say your child walks into the kitchen and points to his sippy cup on the counter and says, "Wawa" (water). You give him the cup and tell him, "Say thank you." But he doesn't. You should promptly pull out the switch and give him a swat, then tell him again, "Say thank you." If he's crying from the swat you just administered, give him a moment to gather himself. Then repeat the command: "Say thank you." If he doesn't obey, immediately swat him again. This may go on for multiple rounds of command and swat, command and swat. It's a test of wills. And his will must be broken. Remember, foolishness is bound up in that will. You must win this battle.

Use training swats to tone down whining, to get your children to eat their food, to keep them from touching something they're not supposed to mess with. Training swats will teach your children to obey at your first command, from a very young age. They are simple, immediate, clear, and effective.

Parents who say, "I've tried spanking, and it doesn't work with my child," are usually not spanking or swatting *hard* enough, *often* enough, *consistently* enough, or *promptly* enough.

Spankings/training swats need to hurt. If they don't, then you're not doing it hard enough. You won't change your children's behavior, and they won't develop any self-control. When you spank properly, there will be a little red mark or two. That's not the end of the world. Hebrews 12:11 teaches us that "For the moment all discipline seems painful rather than pleasant, but later it yields the peaceful fruit of righteousness to those who have been trained by it." This is talking about how God disciplines his children, and the principle is true all the way around: discipline is painful. If it isn't painful, it doesn't work.

Training swats must be frequent. Generally speaking, parents let too much disobedience slide by. They need to spank more. Your toddler will give you many opportunities throughout the day to discipline. Don't let anything go. And don't use spankings as a last resort. Often parents will use every other means of discipline before they spank. But spanking is the clearest way to connect disobedience with pain. (Additionally, other forms of discipline are harder on parents because they require more words, more analysis, and more monitoring, especially if you're using a time-out.) Just swat them.

You must be consistent. Consistency builds trust, which in turn builds respect. It creates a stable home where the rules aren't changed on a whim. And it keeps you from blowing up by keeping things from piling up. We already talked about the importance of consistency for discipline in general—but for training especially, consistency is a must.

Finally, training swats must be prompt. There needs to be an immediate connection in the mind of your toddler between disobedience and pain. Parents are usually too slow to punish. We tend to want to talk it out with our children rather than discipline them. The younger the child, the shorter the interval must be between the act and the consequence. Waiting to spank your two-year-old for a tantrum in Walmart until *after* you finish shopping and *after* you drive home and *after* you put away the groceries will only get you more tantrums next time. If your two-year-old spits on another child, don't delay for even a moment. This is not something that needs conversation. Don't talk to your child about being sweet and loving. Immediately spank your child. The longer you wait to administer a spanking, the less your toddler is able to put two and two together: that this behavior is unacceptable. Don't tell your children, "Wait until your father gets home." Young children have trouble connecting cause and effect. Help them make the connection by spanking promptly.

Expect your children to respect your words.

You should never have to physically force your children to do something. If you, bodily, have to keep their behavior in check, you have a real problem. Your children will get bigger, and you'll only be able to force their hand for so long. Remember, the goal is not simply to get your child to do certain things. The goal is for them to obey you from the heart and to develop self-control. Don't short-circuit their maturity by physically forcing them to obey. Voice commands are all that should be necessary.

For example, if your toddler has something in his hand, and you want him to give it to you, tell him to give it to you. If he doesn't obey, don't take it from his hand. Discipline him. Then ask for it again. It's that simple. Don't grab your child to keep him from running in the house. Call him and tell him to stop—and expect him to obey.

Clarity is key. Make your commands concise and direct. Say things like "Stop," "No," "Put that down," and "Come here." Proverbs 10:19 says, "When words are many, transgression is not lacking." There's a

ERROR 5

REASONING WITH YOUR TODDLER   129

principle in there for parents. Limit your words with your children. The more words, the more confusion. Children are not so fragile that you need to couch every command in soft, flowery language.

On a similar note, don't justify your actions to your toddler. I see this error very frequently. It's such a waste of time. Your toddler doesn't need an explanation. Just discipline him. By rationalizing, you're simply opening yourself up to argument. You're just teaching your children to become better debaters and lawyers. I appreciate the desire parents have for their children to understand moral principles. But as I already mentioned, toddlers aren't old enough to understand abstract reasons— they simply need consistent, prompt discipline. Have those conversations about why we behave in certain ways *when they are at an appropriate age* to grasp those concepts.

If you don't train your child to respect your words in the little things at home, they won't respect your words when it counts. I vividly remember one time we had some friends over to the house, and their son started running toward the street. His mom called (nicely, softly, gently) for him to come back and gave him a list of about eight reasons why he shouldn't be doing what he was doing. But he pressed on toward the road in complete disobedience. My son Bryant was standing there in disbelief at the situation. After a moment, he looked up at

Lisa and said, "Don't worry, I'll go get him," and then took off after the little guy, tackled him, and sat on him until the mom could get down there. This is one of those times the mom should have simply shouted stop. Unfortunately, she wasn't clear or concise with her command, and her son had not been trained to obey. Therefore, physically restraining the child was necessary.

Be clear, concise, and direct. Don't give a command unless you intend for it to be obeyed. And if you give a command that is not obeyed, follow it up with discipline. Expect your child to respect your words.

Fight every battle, win every battle.

When your children are young, you need to fight what might seem like strange battles. Everything is an opportunity to train: eating asparagus, sitting still in church, not talking so much, staying in bed at night, speaking to strangers, etc. Don't let anything pass, no matter how little. A.W. Pink wrote,

> It is of vital importance for the child's future good that he or she should be brought into subjection at an early age. An untrained child means a lawless adult. Our prisons are crowded with those who were allowed to have their own way during their minority. The least offense of a child against the rulers of the home ought not to pass without due correction, for if he finds leniency in one direction or toward one offense, he will expect the same toward others. And then disobedience will become more frequent till the parent has no control except that of brute force.[1]

1. A.W. Pink, "A Word to Parents," *The Ten Commandments* (Grand Rapids: Baker, 1994), 74.

The point here isn't to get your children to eat their vegetables or sleep for eight hours a night. Those are nice byproducts, but the point is to develop self-control and to get your kids in the habit of honoring those in authority. If you will fight the small, everyday battles when your kids are toddlers, you won't have nearly as many battles to fight as they get older. Because one way or the other, you're going to have to fight battles with your children: the question is whether you want to fight those battles when the stakes are low (eat your asparagus) or high (don't date that guy).

Don't make your home childproof. If you want to swap your sharp-edged coffee table for one with rounded corners, that's fine. But don't take away everything you don't want your child to touch. Leave it out, tell your children no, and let the battles begin. And win those battles.

When our kids were little, we'd put a smallish blanket on the floor and put the child in the middle of the blanket with some toys. We'd rub the blanket and say, "Yes." We'd pat the floor area outside the blanket and say, "No." Then we'd sit back, set a timer for fifteen minutes or so, and watch for opportunities to battle with our child's self-will. (Besides being a great way to teach your toddlers self-control, this blanket training can make your home life a lot easier. You can have brief devotions, or cook supper, or clean up the house while your small children sit and play on the blanket.)

ERROR 5
REASONING WITH YOUR TODDLER

If your kids are able to control themselves out-wardly, then they'll be able to control themselves inwardly. If they can control themselves outwardly, then they can control their mind, will, and emotions. Help your toddlers develop self-control by fighting (and winning) every battle.

Don't count.

I hope you don't count to three with your toddler. If you do, make a decision to stop that immediately. Counting allows for slow obedience. And again, slow obedience is disobedience. Parents count to three when their child disobeys, and they know it but won't discipline.

I remember one time we told Bryant to go get himself ready for bed. He simply rolled over and stopped doing what he was doing. It *sort of* looked like obedience. He did quit playing with his toys. But he didn't move toward the bedroom and bathroom and obey what we said to do. If I had counted to three, I would have simply postponed discipline. Don't count to three. Or five. Or ten. This is just another way of training your child to obey only once your voice rises to a certain level.

Shut down temper tantrums.

Never allow temper tantrums. They are the epitome of a child who lacks self-control.

If you have a tantrum-thrower, it's because it works. Your toddler wouldn't throw tantrums if they didn't get him what he wanted. One time we had our friends over at the house. Something happened, and their oldest began kicking and screaming his lungs off in the driveway—but his mom was in the house, oblivious to everything, and it wasn't getting him very much traction. So all of a sudden he stopped, looked at my girls, and said in the clearest and calmest of tones, "Go get my mom." Then he went back to his wailing and gnashing of teeth. Many times a child's behavior is simply a well-orchestrated drama to get what he wants. Remember the saying from earlier: "You get more of what you subsidize and less of what you penalize." Don't give in to temper tantrums, and you'll get fewer of them. They are a blatant challenge to authority—your authority.

What do you do when your toddler throws a temper tantrum in public? Cut your errand short and deal with the problem. You can spank your child right then and there. You can take your child to the bathroom in the store and spank there. You can take him out to the car and discipline him. Your children must know that their obedience is more important to you than your to-do list. Also, realize that poor behavior in public is a sign of poor training in private. A meltdown in the grocery store should make you say to yourself, "I've got to do a better job at home."

One last point: rebellion is not the same thing as frustration. I remember Bryant used to set up battle scenes with plastic army men. If he had trouble getting them to stand up, or if he accidentally knocked some of them over, he'd start crying. Sometimes he'd knock *all* of them over. At first I thought he was throwing a temper tantrum. But then I realized he wasn't really rebelling against his mother or me. He wasn't disobeying us. He was simply frustrated that things weren't working out.

So we tried to change his frustration into something completely different. We reminded him that, while his struggle was no doubt frustrating, it wasn't really something to cry about. Rather, he should cry about the sin in people's hearts and how it comes out in the world in wars, abuse, and theft. We used the situation to show him that there are bigger things in life to consider.

Frustration is a great teaching opportunity, whether your children are struggling to bake a cake, fix a bicycle, or build a fort. Don't step in too quickly. Let them ask for help. Let them learn things on their own. This teaches them to take the initiative in solving problems.

Don't cater.

What toddlers want most is their own way. And parents are very quick to give in. Their children write on walls, talk back to authorities, bounce on the couch, throw toys—and they just kind of laugh it off and say, "What can you do?" I'll tell you what you can do. You can give your children clear boundaries and discipline them when they cross the line.

Teach your toddlers to respect property and people. They should not be allowed to destroy things. They should not be allowed to make fun of someone's hard work. They should not be allowed to physically hurt other children. As they get older, train them to honor older people and give them their seat in a crowded room. Boys should respect girls and treat them in a dignified manner. Your children should not have an "I'm free to do anything I want to do" mentality.

Siblings are tailor-made opportunities in this area. Teach them to respect their sibling's closed door and not to intrude into their time and space. They must ask before borrowing clothes or bicycles. Just because siblings share the same house doesn't mean they can be careless with each other's space and things.

Related to this, many parents seem to think their children will die if they are not catered to at every moment. I'm exaggerating, but not much. Your child will not die if she doesn't have somebody to play with for an afternoon. Your child will not die if you tell him to read a book instead of watch TV. Your child will not die if she doesn't have the newest, nicest shoes. Your child will not die if he goes without a meal. Your child will not die if you make her leave the cousins' house after supper rather than spend the night.

This habit of not catering to your children starts very early, even before they're toddlers. For example, it is very possible to have your children sleep through the night, in their own beds, as early as about six weeks old. All it requires is for you not to cater to their crying in the middle of the night. Don't pick them up to feed them; let them cry it out for a little while, and they will go back to sleep. After two or three nights of this, they will stop crying in the middle of the night and sleep all the way through.

One couple friend of ours, the Longs, had read a book by Dr. Denmark (one of the acknowledgments that I made at the beginning of this book) that recommends this technique. Stacey was less than enthusiastic about letting their firstborn, Lucy, cry it out during the night. But they followed

Dr. Denmark's advice, beginning by loading Lucy up with a full stomach at about ten that night. Her husband, Greg, said he'd be the dutiful husband and get up to check on Lucy—to make sure she wasn't bleeding, caught in her crib, or being attacked by mischievous garden gnomes. He gave Stacey earplugs so she wouldn't hear the wailing and gnashing of teeth. When Lucy woke up, he closed the master bedroom door and went to check on her. After he made sure she was okay, he simply stood outside Lucy's room for the fifteen to twenty minutes it took for her to cry it out. Then she fell back asleep and didn't wake up again until about six in the morning. Stacey was glad things went so well and agreed to have Greg do it again the next night. Lucy woke up again. Greg followed the same routine. That was the last time Lucy woke up in the middle of the night for a feeding. Since then, Greg and Lucy have had two more girls, who also were trained to sleep through the night without any trouble. Having children sleep through the night is possible. But it does require not catering to their every whimper.

The principle needs to be followed not just for getting children to sleep through the night but even more so in the daily affairs of life. If you cater to your toddler's every desire, you'll raise a child who thinks the world revolves around them. Don't do that.

ERROR 5

REASONING WITH YOUR TODDLER

ERROR 6

Neglecting Your
Grade-Schooler

Earlier I noted that parents begin as cops and move to the next stage of being coaches. Parents as cops are attuned to every little behavior—correcting, disciplining, warning, etc. Parents as coaches still provide much of that, but they also move into a mode of explaining, encouraging, and teaching.

The temptation when your kids move from being toddlers to being grade-schoolers is to mistake their new maturity for complete maturity and to stop being vigilant with their discipline as a result. Don't ease off. Keep training them. This shift from being a cop to a coach will *look* like easing off—but you don't ease off so much as shift gears. You change from running your home like a totalitarian police state (as Doug Wilson has called it) to a stage where you and your child talk more, think more, study the Bible more, debrief after activities more, and pray together more. It's a fun stage. It's a rewarding stage.

ACTION

32

Spank.

While grade-schoolers are out of the training swats stage, they still need to be spanked. This is where traditional spankings come into play.

You still need to spank your grade-schooler. But the goal is no longer only to associate disobedience with pain. And being swift to spank is not as necessary now that your child is older. They know what's going on. Instead, you'll be focusing on principles of obedience, forgiveness, and prayer.

The Bible doesn't give us a step-by-step formula for how to spank a grade-schooler. We Brocks had a certain paradigm (below) we tried to follow. Maybe it will be a template you can follow too.

Let's say your child was chasing other children around the sanctuary after church after you told him not to. What steps do you take to deal with this disobedience?

Privacy. When your child disobeys, take him to his bedroom or some other private place. He's old enough now that disciplining him with peers around will be unnecessarily humiliating.

Spank. After getting to a private spot, administer the spanking. I suggest spanking first because it's

ERROR 6
NEGLECTING YOUR GRADE-SCHOOLER 145

better to get it out of the way. That way, your conversation will be heard versus the child not listening for fear of the dreaded spanking to come.

Conversation. After the spanking, talk about the situation. In this example, the disobedience was a direct disregard of your command not to run in church. Explain how this transgressed the word of God. Read the scriptures that call us to different behavior (the fifth commandment, "Honor thy father and mother"; Ephesians 6:1, "Children, obey your parents in the Lord, for this is right"). Remind your child that following the will of the Lord leads to life and joy, while disobedience leads to pain and death.

Heart. Next, you can discuss "the sin behind the sin" that kept him from following the Word of God (the older the child, the easier it is to talk about this deeper concept). Ask your child why he did what he did. His answer will probably be, "I don't know." So what do you do? Keep berating him until he comes up with a better answer? No. *You* tell him why he did what he did. In this example, you could mention that he disobeyed probably because he was more interested in having fun with friends than being sensitive to others. You could suggest that he idolizes popularity and that he wants to be liked by his peers more than he wants to fear the Lord. At the end of the day, he did it because he's a sinner. He did it because sin has turned him in on himself, and now his world revolves around him, and he's selfish, proud, and afraid.

Identity. Remind your child that he is known, loved, and accepted by the Lord. And since he is known, loved, and accepted, he doesn't have to look for that love and acceptance anywhere else.

Put On. Then talk about what he should have done. Help him to see what he should do the next time this type of situation arises. This is very important. Ephesians 4 tells us to "put off your old self" and "put on the new self" (vv. 22, 24). This angle in the conversation ensures that your child recognizes both what he did wrong and what he should have done right. This works itself out in children saying things like, "I was wrong to run in church. What I should have done was _____ (stayed by your side, told Billy not to run in church, asked you if I could go to the playground with Billy)."

Now that he's older, your child must learn to grasp principles, not just rules ("Don't run in church"). Rules change—but if your children understand the "why" behind the rules, they can follow the principle in any situation. Continuing with this example, you want to teach your children not to run in church because older people are nervous they'll get bumped into, fall, and break something. The principle to know and follow is Leviticus 19:32: "You shall stand up before the gray head and honor the face of an old man." If your children grasp this principle of honoring the elderly, then they'll not only stop running in church, they'll give up their seat on a bus or a crowded living room, they'll let an older person go first in line, they'll respect their elders' opinions and listen to them talk about the good ol' days. That's what you want. If your children don't understand the principle, then they'll know not to run in church, sure—but they'll never know why.

Forgiveness. Tell your child that he should ask you to forgive him. He sinned against you by disobeying you. Teach your children to ask, "Will you please forgive me?" Or, if the situation calls for it, they should go to their sibling or older fellow church member or whomever it was they sinned against.

Prayer. End the conversation with prayer. Your child should ask the Lord to forgive him. And he should pray for strength next time to do what is pleasing to God. And you should pray a brief prayer too. A good approach is for you to "dial" and your child to "hang up." If you're only comfortable praying before a meal or praying a rote prayer (such as the Lord's Prayer), ask someone to teach you how to pray extemporaneously. You're going to need that skill in raising children. Pray that God will bless your child with the ability to exercise better self-control. Pray for your child to be less selfish. Pray that he would love his siblings. Your children need to hear you pray, and they need to get in the habit of praying themselves.

Affection. Follow up all of this with a hug. It doesn't have to be a *long* hug—just a brief show of affection will do. Put him in your lap (unless he's too big) while you discuss the events. Hold his hand. If you're not an affectionate person, you have to change. Your child needs a physical display of your love and care. And be sure to tell him that you love him.

I remember being so very impressed and challenged several years ago when I officiated a wedding for a couple. The groom's best man was his dad (not uncommon in the South). The moments prior to the beginning of the ceremony, when the groom, the best man, and I are waiting to enter the sanctuary, are often memorable. This one was particularly memorable because the father and the son displayed such sweet care for each other. They were often hugging and patting each other on the shoulder and back. It was great! I remember thinking to myself that I hope to have that type of love displayed between each of my sons and me when it comes time to watch them get married. Show affection.

After all of this, then what? One thing you can do is have your child sit quietly in his room for a little while (though I'd limit the amount of time he's supposed to sit thinking about his sins). Or you can do nothing and consider the matter closed. This is my preference.

ERROR 6

NEGLECTING YOUR GRADE-SCHOOLER

During the conversation portions of the process outlined above, don't lecture for an extended time. Don't exasperate your child by droning on and on about what he did wrong and should have done right. Keep things brief.

How many swats should you use? That depends on several things. If your child is older, he should probably receive a few more swats. If the offense is severe (spitting on his sibling), the number of swats should also increase; if the offense is minor (slow obedience when you told him to get ready for bed), the number of swats should be minimal. Use common sense here. And regarding the force of the swats, the rule of thumb is simply the more force used, the fewer swats needed. (If you require first-time obedience, the decision about how many swats and how forceful they should be becomes much easier. Rather than having to contend with rising blood pressure and swirling emotions, you'll be able to discipline as objectively as possible.)

The two questions I probably get asked the most are "When do I start spanking my child?" and "When do I stop spanking my child?" I mentioned earlier that training swats can begin at about nine months old. When to stop spanking a child is less clear. This is where knowing your child comes into play, and also general parental wisdom. For younger children, spanking tends to work best. For older children, loss of privileges tends to work best.

It can be quite devastating for an older child (say, ten years old) to get spanked. And keep in mind, administering frequent spankings early (as training swats, to toddlers) should make spanking less necessary as the children grow. There are two principles at play here: (1) discipline must hurt, regardless of the age, and (2) the older the child, the less corporal the punishment.

Use time-outs proactively.

Time-outs can be effective, though they're usually misused. Let me explain. Most parents put their children in time-out after they behave badly. They send their children to their room and tell them to think about what they've done, to change their attitude, to come out when they're ready to apologize, etc. My suggestion is not to send your children away for a time-out *after* they've been bad, but *before*.

When you see your child is starting to unravel, when you can tell that things are going downhill—put him in time-out. Give him the opportunity to get his mind off the situation and settle his emotions. You've probably done something similar yourself after a frustrating morning at work or a difficult conversation with a sibling: you'll take a "time-out" by going for a walk or stepping into the kitchen for a bite to eat. Proactive time-outs help your children remove themselves from potential problems and learn that not every frustrating situation in life can be immediately fixed. Sometimes you simply need to press a reset button on the day or the moment.

Also keep in mind that time-outs are more effective for slightly older children. Time-outs for younger children just create more work for you: if they're out of control around others, what makes you think they'll be calm and quiet while sitting alone? You're just going to have to monitor their behavior from another room. But an older child understands what is going on and can benefit from some time to sit and think. So reserve time-out for somewhat older kids—use it as a slowdown prior to disobedience.

34

Protect your children.

It's tempting to start paying less attention to your kids once they reach an age where they can pretty well fend for themselves. You can't do that. You must continue to protect them. Now that your kids are safe from hot stoves and electrical outlets, you have to be on guard against negative influences that damage their hearts and minds. In 1 Corinthians 15:33, Paul commands us, "Do not be deceived: 'Bad company ruins good morals.'" Earlier in 1 Corinthians, he goes so far as to say, "purge the evil person from among you" (1 Cor. 5:13). Proverbs 13:20 has the same idea: "Whoever walks with the wise becomes wise, but the companion of fools will suffer harm." The Bible recognizes the need to keep your distance from ungodly influences.

Children need protection, first of all, from other kids. Your children's friends might introduce your children to bad attitudes, ungodly music, sexually explicit material, and more. I was first introduced to hard rock music (Led Zeppelin, KISS, and Aerosmith) by neighborhood kids. I first saw teenagers treating parents with open rebellion and disrespect when spending the night with a family friend. I'm embarrassed to say that I first played spin the bottle in about third grade, and I saw my first *Playboy* magazine in fourth or fifth grade. I wasn't led into these things by an adult, nor did I find them at my house (thank you, Dad, for not having this stuff around). I was led into this stuff by other kids close to my age from my neighborhood and school. Parents need to watch out for their kids. Parents need to keep an eye on their kids and protect their innocence for as long as possible.

Children also need protection from perverted and immature adults. In our sexually addicted culture, sexual molestation and pedophilia are on the rise. And sadly, the usual perpetrators of these crimes are family members—uncles, cousins, older brothers, and the like. Parents need to be watchful.

Some parents might choose to protect their children by drawing hard lines, such as not doing sleepovers or not allowing their children to go into a neighbor's home. Others may decide to stay out of youth group activities in favor of activities with other families in the church. Another good way to protect your kids is by making sure siblings are always paired up and doing things together.

Finally, children need protection from cultural influences like TV shows, movies, the internet, advertisements, and music. There are many good resources to guide you through this enormous, complex, and important maze, but here are a few basic principles. (1) Limit your children's exposure to these harmful influences. For example, when we Brocks watched Saturday football, we would often set a timer for the length of a typical commercial break and turn the TV off during that time. (2) Participate with your children as they interact with aspects of modern life. Watch a movie together and talk with them afterward about what sort of worldview was being espoused. Point out how the dad is a doofus in almost every TV show. (3) Surround them with friends who hold similar values. Maybe work a second job so that you can send your kids to a private, Christian school. (4) Pray hard for God's mercy and guiding hand to keep your kids from destructive forces.

In all of this, remember that sin is not something out there somewhere. Sin is in our hearts. As the saying goes in the *Pogo* cartoon, "We have met the enemy, and he is us." Parents should never think that if they can just keep their kids away from the sin out in the world, their kids will automatically grow up godly. Kids will only grow up godly by the power of the Holy Spirit working in their hearts through the means of parents.

Whenever you're confronted by the world's sin, use the encounter as an opportunity. Talk to your children about the need for Jesus. When a sexually graphic commercial pops up on the TV (which it inevitably will), teach your boys to look away. Talk to them about how sad it is that these girls' bodies are being used to sell something. Help them see them as people made in the image of God who have hopes, dreams, and family. Scroll through Instagram and talk with your girls about the sins of envy and comparison, about the danger of curating a life that promotes oneself and creates an image that is not true. Use these sorts of situations as opportunities to pray with your children for those who don't know Christ. But again, don't be the holier-than-thou parent who "just can't believe" what they're seeing. Be the joyful but brokenhearted parent who loves people and hates to see sin destroying lives.

Shut down tattletales.

Most kids tattle because they want to see another kid get in trouble. Don't allow that. Children shouldn't take pleasure in seeing someone else suffer. Hammer that principle home for your children.

One thing you *can* do is teach your children to inform you *before* one of their siblings or friends do something wrong—not to get them in trouble, but to keep them out of it. For example, if your child hears a neighbor kid planning to throw rocks through the windows of a new home that's being built in the area, that would be a good thing to share with his dad. Encouraging this sort of proactive tattling keeps your children focused on the good of their neighbors. It also teaches them to speak up against sin and wrongdoing.

Aside from the above, is tattling ever okay? Yes. Tattling is okay when the child is concerned about the health and safety of the offender. For example, if your child's younger sibling has gotten into the habit of crawling out his window and walking around on the roof, the older sibling should tell her parents, not because she wants to see her kid brother in trouble but because she's concerned he'll get hurt. This is a situation where you have to sense the motives of your child. You need to discipline tattling that is malicious, but you should honor "tattling" when the motive is love.

Tattling is also okay when the child is seeking honest justice, such as when your child tells you who vandalized the school with spray paint. Again, this is a judgment call and sometimes hard to tell. If you pay close attention to your children you should get to the point where you can sense what their true motives are. A good thing about encouraging a child to seek honest justice is that the child learns that it's better to have an authority step in than to take matters into his own hands.

If you have a tattler, remind her what the Bible says: "Vengeance is mine, I will repay, says the Lord" (Rom. 12:19). Dealing with tattletales is a great opportunity to teach our children about the sovereignty of God, the timing of God, and the justice of God.

Cultivate sibling friendship.

Encourage your children to be their siblings' best friends. You want to see them doing things together. You want to see them hanging out in mostly the same groups. You want to see them helping each other, laughing together, and defending each other.

Neighborhood friends and classmates will come and go, but siblings will be related to each other for the rest of their lives. Encouraging siblings to be best friends prioritizes family togetherness and loyalty over giving deference to a clique or peer group. It creates memories, and as we've already talked about, memories bind people together. Sibling friendships force children to learn to work together in harmony and with a long-term view. No one should be able to step in and drive a wedge between family members, siblings in particular.

Siblings will fight. It's inevitable. It goes back to Cain and Abel, Jacob and Esau. So teach your children to resolve their conflicts. It will require intentional practice. It's not natural. Too many parents let their kids "work it out by themselves" with no instruction. The result is resentment, especially in younger, weaker, or outnumbered children. If you make your children demonstrate verbal and physical kindness to each other and absolutely forbid any ill-treatment of siblings, you'll develop a household full of confident children who love each other. And when they move out, they'll form their own homes with similar expectations of what home life should look like.

Here are some of the things you can do to encourage your children to be best friends:

- On birthdays, have them write out "10 Things I Love About _____."
- Train them to be happy for each other when their siblings do well in some effort.
- Have them give Christmas and birthday gifts to their siblings.
- Limit times with peers.
- Make them include each other in activities.
- Make them tell others that their best friend is their sibling.

All of this is not easy. But adult children who have no regrets about how they treated each other growing up and who laugh together, vacation together, and enjoy being around each other is a gift that puts a permanent smile on the face of a parent.

Expect that during the toddler and preschool years, fighting over toys and attention from Mom and Dad will be a regular occurance. A better relationship should start to bud in the elementary-aged years of a child's development. It really should flourish in the teen years. Start early in trying to get your children to be each other's best friends. The Bible says to love your neighbor. For children, siblings are their closest neighbor and first in line for practicing.

ERROR 7

Disrespecting
Your Teenager

Teenagers look like adults. They begin to act like adults too (driving cars, working jobs, having romantic interests). When you treat your teenagers like children, you disrespect them and undercut your ability to influence their lives. When you attempt to control their lives like you did when they were young, you show disrespect for your teenager. Teenagers are young adults, and you must begin treating them like young adults.

Remember, when your children are toddlers, you're a cop, and when they're grade-schoolers, you're a coach. But now that your kids are teenagers, you need to become a counselor. There will still be some discipline involved, though not in the form of spankings. At this point, the bulk of a parent's responsibilities is to help their children *see* and *understand*: *see* different options for the way issues could be handled and *understand* reasons why or why not to take certain actions.

Parents should talk often with their grade-school kids—but those "coach" conversations are heavily one-sided, with the parents doing most of the talking. With teens, there should be a lot of two-way conversation.

By parenting as a counselor when your children are in the teen years, you show them great respect. You treat them as an adult, and they appreciate it. Listening to them endears you to them. Not interrupting them or speaking in a condescending way opens up lines of communication that they desperately need. They need your wisdom because, even though their bodies may look mature, their brains are still lagging behind.

Parenting teenagers has the potential to be an incredibly enjoyable time. No, you won't be best friends yet (that comes later), but you'll start to laugh together, talk about theology and politics together at a deep level, and enjoy activities together. It's fantastic!

Don't imitate your teenager.

A big temptation for parents of teenagers is to respond to them the way they respond to you. This is another situation where the principle that *parenting begins with parents* comes into play. You have the opportunity to do unto your teenagers as you would have them do unto you—rather than doing unto them *as* they do unto you.

As children get older, they want to be seen as mature, independent, and capable. They shy away from their parents; they don't want to be seen with them; they don't want to talk to them. We all did that, didn't we? Don't take it so personally. Your child is learning independence. If you need your children to need you, you're going to have a hard time during the teenage years. Teens are bigger and adult-looking, so you expect them to act like it—but they won't! They go through a physical maturation process in short order, but the social, emotional, and mental maturation process takes a long time. They're still young and insecure. So were you. Treat them gently and with respect.

Don't avoid your teenager the way he or she avoids you. Don't clam up and get snarky with your teenager the way he or she might get with you. (By the way, if you discipline your children consistently when they're young, you should have much fewer displays of disrespect when they're older.) Be diligent to continue to listen to them and make time for them. Keep working to train them up in the nurture and admonition of the Lord. Don't stop talking to them, even when it seems they couldn't care less about what you're saying. They're listening to more than you think.

I remember hearing about a youth minister who was simply making some phone calls to chat with his youth. He called one kid who was new to the group and whom he didn't know very well. He called and talked with the guy and got the typical teenager response: few words, monotone voice, mumbling, and seemingly complete disinterest. The youth minister got off the phone and thought something like, "He doesn't like me or the youth group; he'll probably never be back." But a week or so later, the youth minister saw the kid's mom, and she profusely thanked the youth minister for calling. She mentioned how much her son appreciated it and felt included, and how he was so smiley and happy afterward. While the kid was on the phone, he acted like he couldn't care less about the conversation. But internally, he was ecstatic.

Teenagers won't give you any feedback. So don't expect it. They won't tell you what a great mom or dad you are. They won't tell you how much they appreciate you talking to them. They won't tell you how grateful they are for the way you raised them. Just keep talking to your kids. Though they may not appear the least bit interested, they're hearing every word.

38

Respect your teenager's private world.

Your child's private world is that inner chamber where their thoughts, dreams, and fears reside. It's a place they rarely speak of. It's a place you might not even know exists.

To respect your child's private world is to honor those thoughts, dreams, and fears. It's to appreciate them and not mock them. It's to listen with patience rather than jump in with comments. When your teenager tells you about a romantic interest and you joke about young love or Romeo and Juliet, you're not respecting their tender thoughts and feelings. An athletic mom who rolls her eyes at her academic daughter is not respecting her private world. Be sure of this: if you don't treat your child's deeper thoughts and feelings carefully when they open up to you, they will not open up to you again.

There will be occasions where your child invites you into their private world. Be ready to listen. I repeat: LISTEN. If you jump into your child's self-disclosure with your words and opinions, you'll shut him or her down. So shut up. Quit talking.

ERROR 7
DISREPECTING YOUR TEENAGER 169

Maybe ask a leading question or two, such as "How did that make you feel when . . . ?" or "When did this first happen?" Those types of questions are good. They show you're interested in your child. But don't start talking—especially about yourself. Listen. Don't lecture, listen.

Parents, you'll have to quit being so distracted to make this happen. If you're so busy with work or watching TV or scrolling, you'll miss these opportunities. My teenagers tended to open up about the time I was ready to go to sleep. Our older two girls would show up in our room at bedtime and sit around and talk. They'd be sitting on the bed I was wanting to crawl into. But they'd be talking. The topics would range all over: boys, colleges, schoolwork, church, etc. If we had insisted on maintaining a decent bedtime, we'd have missed those opportunities. I'm not sure what it is about nighttime, but that's when teenagers start to open up. So go sit on their bed for a minute, ask a good open-ended question, and listen. (If you're an early bird by nature, you may have to make some adjustments to your life.) Here are a few good open-ended questions that help lead to good conversations with teens:

- What are you frustrated about these days?
- What about (name a friend) do you really like? What annoys you?

- What's your favorite thing about our church? Least favorite?

- When did you recently have a really good laugh?

- What are your thoughts about (name a current event)?

- What brings you the most joy these days?

If your teen has rebelled, I'm sorry that you've had a hard time with your child. The place to begin to win back their heart is with your confession of sin and repentance. A great time to do this is when you're in a good, deep conversation (probably at night). This is not a guarantee that your prodigal child will return to you, but it is the place to start. Talk to your child and admit your sins and ask your child to forgive you.

Let your teenager make mistakes.

I talked earlier about letting consequences be the punishment for children. This is especially important for teenagers. Let them learn from their mistakes.

Curtis Tanner, one of the founders of Campus Outreach, has had a big impact on my life. I remember Curtis telling me that when his son turned sixteen, he was going to give him a chunk of money: one thousand dollars or so. His son would be free to do whatever he wanted with it. Why? Curtis said that a sixteen-year-old with a little bit of money can only make little mistakes, while an older child with more money can make big mistakes. Curtis wanted to give his son the opportunity to fail while he was still very much in the picture and able to help him think through things.

This makes sense to me. As your kids get older, give them freedom. Let them try things and learn. Let them make mistakes and deal with the consequences. Let them have fun.

This all goes back to how you have to change positions as a parent. You must let loose as your kids grow older. If you don't, they'll grow bitter because they can't keep all your rules. Randy Alcorn wrote this:

> Our kids need us to not only raise the bar high for them—and make no mistake, they do need that—but also to believe the best of them, being quick to affirm and offer grace when they stumble. This will help them not to give up because they think they can't please us, and therefore can't please God. . . . May your children see in you the Jesus who came "full of grace and truth."[1]

You invite rebellion if you squash a teen's growing sense of independence. Allowing them to suffer the consequences of their own decisions gives them the sense of confidence and independence that they need. It also gives them a new appreciation for you, since you're allowing them to live and make decisions rather than continuing to treat them like a two-year-old.

I appreciate what Michael and Debi Pearl wrote in their book *Jumping Ship*:

> Some parents settle for too little, controlling only the outward behavior of their children,

1. Randy Alcorn, "When It Comes to Parenting Your Teenage Children, No One Can Take Your Place," Eternal Perspective Ministries, January 15, 2020, https://www.epm.org/resources/2020/Jan/15/parenting-teenage-children.

ERROR 7
DISRESPECTING YOUR TEENAGER 173

but not equipping their souls. They are forceful in their discipline and do indeed train their younger children to obey at home and perform well in public, but fail to equip them with independent decision-making skills and character. You can keep children in baby seats and later belt them into wheelchairs so they will not fall down and break a limb, a sure guarantee of their safety, but it will not teach them to run with the ball and get back up after suffering the hard knocks that life will throw their way. Children will not be content to be protected and guarded. If you squeeze too hard, they will slip out of your grasp as sure as a wet bar of soap.[2]

2. Michael and Debi Pearl, *Jumping Ship: What to Do So Your Children Don't Jump Ship to the World When They Get Older* (Pleasantville, TN: No Greater Joy Ministries, 2007), 40–41.

Make sure your teenager has good friends.

Remember, 1 Corinthians 15:33 reads, "Do not be deceived: 'Bad company ruins good morals.'" Proverbs 13:20 teaches us that "whoever walks with the wise becomes wise, but the companion of fools will suffer harm." And Psalm 1 agrees: "Blessed is the man who walks not in the counsel of the wicked, nor stands in the way of sinners, nor sits in the seat of scoffers." I remember hearing years ago that "ten years from now you'll be pretty much the exact same person you are today except for two things: the books you read and the people you hang around." Your friends greatly affect the trajectory of your life.

Teenagers are generally very focused on what their friends think. What matters most to your teenagers is where their friends are and what they are doing. This change in priorities can happen fast. I remember feeling bewildered when my first two children went from caring about what Mom and Dad thought to seemingly forgetting about us completely. It was like a light switch—one day all that mattered to them was their friends.

ERROR 7

This is a very natural stage of life that kids go through (upon reflection, I realized I went through the exact same thing). So do all that you can to foster positive peer influences. Do your best to make church and other Christian organizations the place where your kids spend a lot of time and develop their closest friends.

My best friends in high school were from the church I attended. Many of them actually went to rival schools (though my very best friend, Tim, did go to the same school as me). We were friends because of the bond of the Holy Spirit. We prayed together, did street evangelism together, sang in choir together, and called each other "knucklehead" whenever any of us started to stray from the Lord. We hung out all weekend. We pulled pranks on each other. There were kids from non-Christian homes who became a part of our group, and it transformed their lives for the good. Many of them are still walking with God today, including several who are doing full-time Christian ministry work. I'm very thankful for those friends and that youth group. The teen years are years when peer influences are strong. Do all you can to help those influences be good ones.

While I just said, "do all you can" to enable your children to have good influences, one thing I think you can't do is change churches for your teenager. I've seen many parents leave the church they've been a part of for many years because the church down the street has a better youth group. This type of disloyalty is not something you want to model for your children. You exemplify the beauty of commitment when you stay true to your home church despite it not being as flashy as others. You don't want to communicate to your teenager that you will totally rearrange your life just so they can sit with their friends in Sunday morning worship or go to a youth Sunday School class.

One philosophy I appreciate is when parents tell their teenagers that the church that has been their "family church" for many years will continue to be their family church, even though the youth group is weak or nonexistent. Sometimes these parents will allow their teens to attend another church's youth activities, so long as the other church agrees with the family's theological perspective. I think this is a decent compromise, a way to recognize a teenager's interest in peers while encouraging the teen to deny himself and show loyalty to the family.

ACTION

Point your children to Christ.

The final brief thing I want to say regarding parenting teens is this: work hard to keep your children from finding their identity and security in things other than the Lord Jesus Christ. If they're Christians, they've been bought by the blood of the Lamb and made citizens of a new kingdom. Nothing should rival that status.

The teen years are when your child starts to accept certain ideas on their own. They start to come to conclusions about God, man, sin, and salvation. They start to solidify their ideas about themselves and the world. You must encourage them to rest in the love of God and to believe the promises of God's Word.

I told the story earlier about the twin who went off the reservation after he stopped playing football. This is the kind of thing we must avoid with our children. They can't be known as the star athlete, or the beauty queen, or the brilliant mind. They need to find their lives in Jesus.

And this leads to the final chapter of this book.

ERROR

Missing Christ

I don't think I have all the answers. As I've said before, most of the material in this book is not original to me. Most of it comes from the individuals I listed in the acknowledgments. And I know that many godly, obedient, respectful children have come from homes where parents raised their kids somewhat differently from what I'm promoting in these pages. As a result, most of my advice up to this point has been suggestions, ideas, and things that worked for us.

But the issues that I'm going to address here at the conclusion of this book speak to ultimate matters. You can fail in many ways as a parent, but you want your prayer to be, "Lord, please don't let me fail to pass along a love for Christ Jesus to my children. If they get only one thing from me, may it be the lordship of Jesus Christ over every area of life."

42

Display Christ.

It's very possible for parents to follow all of the principles in this book or some other book and raise children who are obedient, respectful, and decent citizens yet do not follow the Lord. Don't think that your child is born again just because he is obedient at your first command and follows the interrupt rule. You may have a child who appreciates your authority but doesn't appreciate the Scriptures. You may have a really nice kid who is still enslaved to his sin. Do all you can to see that your children love Christ.

Here are a few characteristics I've seen in Christian homes that failed to produce children who love the Lord. This is not an automatic kind of thing. Plenty of young people come to Christ and walk with God for a lifetime who grew up in homes where these unfortunate characteristics are present. The Spirit of God is powerful to save despite our many displays of these characteristics (thanks be to God!). But *anger*, *legalism*, *flippancy*, and *hypocrisy* are serious actions and attitudes that we must strive to avoid.

Parental *anger* ruins the hearts of children. Anger is traumatic and unnerving. No one likes to be around someone when they're angry. Parents who consistently display anger will cause their children to run far from them and the things they value (or, at least, say they value). Whether that anger is obvious (toe-to-toe yelling at your teenager) or more inconspicuous (constant disappointment about your children's performance in school or failure to make the baseball team), parental anger can cause long-term problems for your children.

I never thought of myself as an angry person. But I remember one day it hit me that I had to develop self-control in this area. I was giving my girls a bath one night after supper. As they were splashing around and getting some water out of the tub, and also on me, doing what typical four-year-olds and two-year-olds do in a bathtub, I balled up my fists and clenched my teeth, and my head began shaking back and forth while I held my tongue. But my oldest saw me, and it greatly scared her. It scared me too! I didn't realize that there was an under-current of anger inside. I remember praying and asking the Lord to forgive me and give me more grace and patience. Thankfully, he has answered that prayer. As I've already said, parenting begins with parents.

Many young parents tell me about their struggles with anger. Often with men it results in them clamming up for a time and eventually blowing up, expressing it in punching a wall or leaving the house and going for a drive. Women will frequently let loose by raising their voice at their children. But the fruit of the Spirit is self-control. Beg the Lord to make you one who, like Christ, exemplifies poise and restraint.

Legalism is another deterrent to your children following Christ. The type of legalism I most often encounter in Christian homes is teaching the commandments of men as the doctrines of God (Matt. 15:9). I refer to this as "fence-building" legalism. Fence-building legalism looks at God's settled law, and then erects fences around it to make sure no one even gets close to breaking it. For example, say a family establishes a rule against drinking alcohol because it might lead to drunkenness, which is clearly forbidden in the Bible. But the drinking of alcohol itself is never forbidden; in a couple of places, it's even encouraged (1 Tim. 5:23; Ps. 104:15). There is usually some wisdom in these fences that we build. There is usually an admirable zeal for the Lord. But this sort of persnicketiness is not biblical, and for children, it often is a major source of exasperation and disdain.

By the way, I don't think I've ever seen legalism that wasn't accompanied by anger. The two almost always go together. Usually a great amount of self-righteousness—"God, I thank you that I am not like other men" (Luke 18:11)—accompanies this form of legalism as well.

ERROR 8
MISSING CHRIST

Flippancy also hinders your children from following Christ. Being glib and superficial about the things of God (also known as not fearing the Lord) will produce children who only show their faith card in social situations where it is to their advantage. If you read your Bible rarely, pray rarely, skip Lord's Day worship because you had a busy week, and are constantly consuming worldliness through social media and laughing about it, you're taking the Lord's name in vain, because you're taking the name of Christian but not acting like it. You're being flippant and careless about the lordship of Christ. If you don't take your faith seriously, why should your children?

This lackadaisicalness is just the opposite of the legalism I wrote about above. Being lackadaisical often flows from a fear of appearing overly zealous for God. We want to be respected by the world, so we avoid coming across as a dedicated, fervent fearer of God. Many times for us Christians, the highest compliment we could receive is to hear the world say, "You don't act like a fundamentalist." And we will compromise our commitment to Christ to secure that accolade. God deliver us from such a man-pleasing mindset!

Finally, *hypocrisy* is sure to turn your children away from you and the things of God. Everyone is inconsistent at times in having their walk match their talk. But a lifetime of portraying yourself as a godly and spiritually-minded person and then bullying the server at the local restaurant, bragging about the good deeds you performed, and lying about your child's age so that you can get the "kids under eight are free" discount will cause your children to run in the opposite direction of you and God. They may grow up and treat you in a civil manner, but they won't love the things you purport to love.

On the other side of the coin, here are a few characteristics of the homes I've seen where the kids grew up with a lifelong affection for the Lord: *love*, *humility*, and *prayer*.

Love covers a multitude of sins (1 Pet. 4:8). Tender affection for your children, along with an unwavering commitment to them no matter how far short they fall, will endear them to you and to the things you stand for. Love shows itself in sacrifice. When your children see that you sacrifice yourself and put them first, they will be secure in your love; they will sense it deeply. This sacrifice might look like picking them up late at night from a junior high church event when you'd rather be in bed asleep. It might look like altering your work schedule so that you can be home more with the kids. It might look like pushing them hard when they want to quit—sometimes love is tough. It might look like simply lending a listening ear rather than a lecture when they tell you about a frustrating friendship at school. Love never fails (1 Cor. 13:8).

ERROR 8

MISSING CHRIST

Humility is another character trait that draws your children to you and the God you serve. God is opposed to the proud but gives grace to the humble (James 4:6). A humble parent admits when he is wrong. A humble parent asks his children to forgive him when he sins against them or in front of them. Again, God gives grace to the humble. The humble also receive the favor and respect of their children.

Finally, *pray*! Paul tells us to "pray without ceasing" (1 Thess. 5:17). Jesus taught his disciples the parable of the persistent widow, "to the effect that they ought always to pray and not lose heart" (Luke 18:1). One of the greatest things we can do for our kids is pray for them. Not to pray is to say, subconsciously, that we don't need God. Paul Miller has written, "If you are not praying, then you are quietly confident that time, money, and talent are all you need in life. You'll always be a little too tired, a little too busy. But if, like Jesus, you realize you can't do life on your own, then no matter how busy, no matter how tired you are, you will find the time to pray."[1] Children need parents who pray.

My parents became Christians later in life (they were in their mid-thirties). They still had some rough spots on them. But I didn't doubt that they prayed. I often saw them having personal devotions.

1. Paul Miller, *A Praying Life: Connecting with God in a Distracting World* (Colorado Springs: NavPress, 2009), 49.

I appreciated that about them. I wanted to provide that same kind of model for my kids.

You can't be satisfied with moral kids. Many non-Christians raise kids who follow biblical morals and live decent lives. Don't expect your children to come to know the Lord easily or automatically just because you disciplined them consistently. Urge your children to believe; talk to them about daily repentance and faith; help them to see the privileges and responsibilities they must grow up into as a result of being a part of the covenant community. And give them a sincere, genuine example of what all of that looks like.

Teach the whys.

If you only teach your children to obey because you said so, they will never know the principle behind the command. In life, your children will need an internal compass to guide them. They must know why they're doing what they're doing. To quote the Ezzos, "A major reason children do not internalize values is because parental instruction too often lacks moral reason."[1]

A child who has not internalized biblical values is susceptible to the temptations and pressures that will come his way. Hosea 4:6 tells us, "My people are destroyed for lack of knowledge." How will your six-year-old respond when all of the other kids are running in church? What will your eight-year-old say to his basketball team when they ask him why he won't play travel ball and be gone all weekend? What will your twelve-year-old do if his friends shove a smart phone with a picture of a naked woman into his face? Teaching the whys is crucial to your children internalizing biblical standards.

1. Gary and Anne Marie Ezzo, *Parenting from the Tree of Life: Leader's Guide*, 2nd ed. (Simi Valley, CA: Growing Families International, 2019), 47.

When Bryant was about ten or eleven, he wanted to quit the basketball team. He didn't play very much. He rode the bench. And he wanted to stop. I could have just told him no. And Bryant, who is an obedient and respectful son, wouldn't have pushed back. The case would have been closed, and he would have finished the season. But I decided to tell him *why* I wouldn't let him quit. I told him that one of the duties of life is to persevere through difficulties and that this was a good opportunity to push through, even though it wasn't enjoyable—in other words, this was good practice for life down the road. I told him that one of the attributes of a Christian man is that you must do hard things, say hard things, do unpopular things. I talked about how you don't quit something just because you're not the best at it or because you might fail. In much of life, you won't be the best (athlete, husband, father, architect, Christian), but you stay at it and keep getting up when you fall down. I preached a little sermon to him. I told him why I said no to his request. He stayed on the team. And I think he's a better man today for it.

This matter of teaching the whys is essential. Your child will encounter all kinds of circumstances in life, and knowing the whys—the principles—is crucial. They need to internalize biblical standards. They will do this best when they know why they should hold to those standards.

ERROR 8

MISSING CHRIST

44

Honor the church.

A great way to turn your children away from the Lord is to roll your eyes at church and scoff at fellow Christians. So many parents teach their children to treat church like a waste of time by griping about how they feel hurt by the church or how they don't like certain individuals.

If you want to keep your children positive and optimistic about the bride of Christ, keep your thoughts to yourself when you think the preaching is boring, the music minister is cheesy, or the youth director is nerdy. If you want to help your children develop a growing faith and love for fellow Christians, don't hop from one church to another. Stay put and work through issues. Stay in church year after year and watch your children take hold of your values and make them their own.

For the Christian, the church is central. It's like a magnet—and your children, if they're born again and in Christ, will always be drawn to it. It's part of being a Christian. Do not give them a bad attitude about the church by passing along your bad attitude about the church. Don't give them unrealistic expectations about the church by passing along your unrealistic expectations about the church. Don't warp their love for fellow believers by passing along your lack of love for fellow believers.

This goes back once more to our first theme: *parenting begins with parents*. The bottom line is that the apple doesn't fall far from the tree. Your kids will view the church the way you view the church. If you spoil their love for it, you warp a central aspect of their life forever. If you give your children an appreciation for the bride of Christ, they will stay attached to her, receiving from her the nourishment that is promised through Word and sacrament (Rom. 10:17; 1 Cor. 10:16).

Practically speaking, never give the impression that church is optional. School is not optional. Why should church be optional? Staying up late on Saturday night does not give you permission to skip worship. Neither does having an invitation to do something on Sunday morning. Talk with your children about their disappointments with your church. They need wisdom from you regarding how to think about the sin they will see and experience. And lastly, pray with your children for your church. Help them learn compassion for others' weaknesses. Help them learn to trust God's sovereignty. Guide them in having a desire to work proactively for your church's improvement.

Help your children know their hearts.

We're governed by what we worship. We worship whatever we think will provide the security, peace, love, and acceptance we lost in the Garden of Eden. And whenever that god is threatened, we protect it. We get angry and controlling. We harden our hearts. We lie, cheat, and steal. Therefore, the quickest way for us to overcome sin is to see the idols in our hearts. Only then will we look to the true God, who alone can provide all the security, peace, love, and acceptance that our souls are on a mission to discover.

Children also need to have the false idols of their hearts exposed. When you see ungodly behavior in your kids, they're showing you that they worship something other than the Lord—just like when you see ungodly behavior in yourself, you're revealing that you worship something other than the Lord. It has been said that you only break commandments two through ten after you break commandment one. In other words, you only steal, for example, because something other than the Lord himself has become the top priority in your life.

ERROR 8
MISSING CHRIST

Parents are responsible to help their children recognize their idols. Say your child threw rocks through a car window. You must start asking, "Why?" When you do, you'll realize there are multiple reasons why your child might do this.

Let's run down one possible pathway: your child threw rocks through the car window because of peer pressure. Why did your child fall to the pressure of peers? The answer is most likely that your child wants to please these friends more than anyone else: more than parents, more than God, more than other friends who aren't vandalizing cars. Why does he want to please his disobedient friends more than anyone else? Probably because at some point in the recent past he has been accepted and loved by that group of kids—they have provided something that your child is looking for. Most likely your child has some wrong thinking about what it means to be accepted and loved. It's your job to get him to think correctly about what love, acceptance, peace, and security actually are.

You might be thinking: Isn't it the job of a pastor or a therapist to work through this kind of stuff with your child? They can be a great resource. That's what churches, youth ministries, and counseling centers do (or should do). But ultimately, you're the one with the most influence over your child's life. You're the one who is around him every day. You're the one who really knows his personality and temperament. You're the one who needs to speak into his life, lead him away from false idols, and lead him toward the one true, living God made manifest in Jesus of Nazareth.

Your children won't be able to answer many of these "Why?" questions that you'll ask. That's part of being a child, and part of the reason they need parents. So when you ask them why they did something and they say, "I don't know," don't keep pushing for an answer. Instead, *you* tell them why they did it. It's your job to know them better than they know themselves. Help them to see the idols of their hearts.

The only way to real and lasting change is to replace our idols with the true God himself. Scottish Presbyterian minister Thomas Chalmers (1780–1847) argues in his sermon "The Expulsive Power of a New Affection" that we can't simply tell ourselves to stop sinning. We need to direct our desires away from the false satisfaction of sin and toward that which truly satisfies and liberates: God himself. Chalmers says that moralism cannot motivate men and women to live properly. Moralism may disparage the vanity and hollowness of the world. It makes the folly of the world thoroughly obvious. But still nothing changes. In order for our hearts to actually change, we need a "new affection," which we get at conversion. Chalmers puts it this way: "The only way to dispossess [the heart]

ERROR 8
MISSING CHRIST

of an old affection, is by the expulsive power of a new one."[1]

This new affection is beautiful. We are impure and needy—but Jesus ministered to impure and needy people, like the woman at the well (John 4:1–42). We are sinners—but Paul says, "God shows his love for us in that while we were still sinners, Christ died for us" (Rom. 5:8). We are ignorant and deceived—but Jesus prayed on the cross, "Father, forgive them, for they know not what they do" (Luke 23:34). These pictures of God's love for sinners builds a new affection in us that expels the heart of old, empty affections.

Sin always produces guilt. This means that our children will always be pining for a word of grace and forgiveness. Let's go back to the car vandalism example. After helping your child see that he sinned because he worships his peers, remind him that idolatry is a great sin punishable by death, but Jesus paid the price of death in his place. Therefore your child has the smile of God upon him. And if you have the smile of God upon you, you don't need the smile of ungodly friends.

Say your child stole a sibling's toy and accidentally broke it. Talk to her about how her need for

---

1. Thomas Chalmers, "The Expulsive Power of a New Affection," Monergism, accessed March 6, 2024, https://www.monergism.com/thethreshold/sdg/Chalmers,%20Thomas%20-%20The%20Exlpulsive%20Power%20of%20a%20New%20Af.pdf.

ERROR 8
MISSING CHRIST

that toy probably stems from discontentment with her own toys. She idolizes possessions and believes that *things* will satisfy her. But Jesus was punished in her place, and not only that, he lived a perfectly righteous life and credits it to her account so that the love the Father has for him is passed on to her.

This is how you bring up your children in the nurture and admonition of the Lord. Teach them about their sin and their heart idols. Teach them about their Savior. Take them to the cross and give thanks for Jesus. Reminding your children that they are known, accepted, and adopted by God will motivate them to live a life of righteousness for the Lord. Parents must help their children see the idols of their heart and the beauty of the cross.

Parents who know the love of God rest in that love; they rest in the forgiveness that is theirs in Christ. And they display love and forgiveness and peace and joy in their parenting. Therefore, it goes back to our first principle one last time: parenting begins with parents.

Remember God's mercy and grace for you.

You won't perfectly train your children. You will make every mistake in the book. There is no fool-proof parenting philosophy—and even if there were, none of us would perfectly implement it. Every parent will have regrets.

When my oldest daughter, Ragan, went off to college, I spent the days leading up to her send-off thinking, "I've not prayed with her enough. I've not had enough one-on-one time with her. I've not talked about dating and relationships in a thorough enough manner. I've not been consistent enough in our family devotions. I've not properly discipled her and taught her the best ways to have personal devotions. I've not celebrated her achievements enough. I've not had her get enough time with older, godly mentors. I've not been on enough mission trips with her." On and on the list of regrets went. I couldn't get my failures and mistakes out of my head.

What do you do when you're struck by the reality of your failures? The common way to deal with

ERROR 8
MISSING CHRIST

these mistakes and regrets is to try to convince yourself that you're not that bad. You did have some family devotions, you did have some one-on-one time, you did go on a mission trip with her, etc. But that's a shallow attempt to deal with your regrets. It's the world's way of thinking, frankly. The world wants you to try to convince yourself that you're not too bad.

The reality is that you're worse than you realize. Not only did you fail in all the ways you can think of, but you failed (and continue to fail) in tons of other ways you don't even know about. Bad attitudes that you passed on to your children. Inconsistencies in your life that confuse your children. Misplaced values that your children can't shake. The list could go on and on with ways you've failed your kids.

So what do you do? You take all that to the cross. You lay it all at the feet of Jesus. You say to Jesus the words of the hymn "Rock of Ages":

> Not the labors of my hands
> Can fulfill Thy law's demands;
> Could my zeal no respite know,
> Could my tears forever flow,
> All for sin could not atone;
> Thou must save, and Thou alone.
>
> Nothing in my hand I bring,
> Simply to the cross I cling;

Naked, come to Thee for dress;
Helpless look to Thee for grace;
Foul, I to the fountain fly;
Wash me, Savior, or I die.

The solution to our guilt is the blood and righteousness of Jesus. The way to peace, security, and gladness of heart is not to convince yourself that you're not that bad, but to trust that the blood and righteousness of Jesus covers your failures, mistakes, and sins.

Rest in Jesus. Rest in God's sovereignty. God draws straight lines with crooked sticks, and every parent is a crooked stick. He works through you to accomplish his goals. And He will continue to work toward his goals for you and your children. He never makes mistakes. His timing is perfect. His power is great. All his ways are right. Trust him.

After dropping Ragan off at college, when I was alone (I can't remember if it was later that night or early the next morning), I found myself giving praise to God for his grace that is greater than all my sin. This is the gospel for Christian parents. The gospel frees you from wallowing in guilt and regret. The gospel tells you to walk out into the world as a forgiven child of God with joy and a smile on your face. Parenting is a wonderful thing!

ERROR 8
MISSING CHRIST

Appendix: The List

Made in the USA
Monee, IL
25 July 2024

62632607R00132